THE OBSERVER'S BOOK OF

ARCHITECTURE

Written and Illustrated by
JOHN PENOYRE, A.R.I.B.A.
and
MICHAEL RYAN, F.R.I.B.A.

Foreword by
F. R. S. YORKE, F.R.I.B.A.

Describing and Indexing the
DEVELOPMENT OF BUILDING IN BRITAIN
from Saxon times to the present day
with over 250 illustrations, many
of which are coloured

FREDERICK WARNE & CO. LTD.
FREDERICK WARNE & CO. INC.
LONDON · NEW YORK

AUTHORS' PREFACE

To MANY PEOPLE architecture is something special; it refers to a type of building which is grandiose, a church or a town hall; it could never refer to the house they live in, though, strangely, there are many among the same people who would invite an architect to build a house for them. Is there not a paradox here? What has become of a house designed by an architect if it is not architecture? The truth is that it *is* architecture. The word itself has only become stilted in its meaning.

In this book we have attempted to put this word Architecture into perspective. We have written not so much for those already interested as for the layman who, unwittingly, lives with architecture round him every day. We hope that he will become aware of it, observe it and understand it for what it is. It is more than mere building. It is an actual record of true history, not only of bricks and mortar but of human lives and habits.

This realisation of architecture is valuable. It puts before us the proper view of architecture, relating our own times to modern developments in building. It explains the new shapes which are evolving today and it brings back to this country an architecture which is vigorous and alive.

We have been encouraged by the popularity of our first edition to add to this one an illustrated glossary of technical terms for the benefit of the majority to whom these terms are not familiar. We have also revised the whole of the chapter on the twentieth century.

4

FOREWORD

ARCHITECTURE IN any age is conditioned by the contemporary system of economy, methods of production, and requirements of society; but it has its roots in the past. This is not to say that any great architecture is a reproduction of the work of an earlier period, but that the sense of scale and proportion and the handling of the texture and colour of building materials are not invented afresh by every generation. They come partly from the inspiration we get from new demands and the new methods we have for meeting them, and partly from the rich legacy of building tradition.

It is important, if we are to get a full enjoyment from observing the architecture of this or any former time, that we should know something of the conditions on which the style is founded.

In this stimulating and extraordinarily well-balanced book Penoyre and Ryan have traced quite clearly—so clearly that I found it possible to understand the text without the diagrams—the development of English architecture from Saxon times, and have provided just the background that the observer needs to help him follow, without confusion or bogging down in unnecessary detail, the development of building, planning, and technique through the centuries; and that should help, too, to get rid of some of the misgivings he may have about the architecture of today.

F. R. S. Y.

5

CONTENTS

CONTENTS

FULL PAGE ILLUSTRATIONS

7

INTRODUCTION

ARCHITECTURE IMPLIES building beautifully and well. Great architecture can be profoundly moving, can stir us more deeply than any other of the visual arts, for it is a three-dimensional art into which the beholder may enter and of which he may feel himself to be an integral part. Architecture is not the application of beautiful detail to a building; to aspire to the name of architecture the building itself must not only be well built but must truly fulfil its purpose and at the same time delight the beholder.

The factors that govern the form of any building are three—its purpose, or the needs of the builders; the skill of the builders themselves, in which we include their knowledge and traditions; and the materials that are most readily available. Since social needs and technical skill both change in time with the history of the country, and since it is to the progressive change of social condition that architecture owes its changing form in different ages, this review is treated chronologically.

Primarily, this is a reference book, designed specifically to give the observer the information he wants in a form easily remembered. Buildings of various periods look as they do for very definite reasons, and these reasons are explained as far as possible in the text; but their actual appearance and basic characteristics are less easily explained in words. They must be illustrated, even caricatured, if their qualities are to be fully appreciated.

Hence the majority of the illustrations in this book are not exact representations of particular

ELY FROM THE SOUTH-EAST

buildings; they are generalisations of essentials. Their colours, too, are decorative and diagrammatic rather than realistic, and form some aid to memorising the characteristics of the main architectural periods: for example, Blue for the Decorated and Perpendicular Gothic or Yellow for the transitional styles of Tudor and Elizabethan. The comparatively few full-page illustrations do not always follow this principle which in some instances has been sacrificed to realism.

At the end of the book will be found an index—again wholly illustrative in character—which has been called the Visual Index. Its purpose is to group together certain features (doors, columns, etc.) in such a way that the observer, when faced with a building for identification, may note for himself its peculiar elements, compare them to their equivalents or approximate equivalents in the Visual Index, and then refer to the text as indicated.

In the first section of the Index, Architectural Character, an attempt has been made to illustrate the atmosphere and the "feeling" of the various periods without reference to particular details, as it is found that general character is often of paramount importance in the identification of periods.

The Index, however, must be used with some caution, for the presence of details that belong to a specific period by no means ensures that the building in which they occur actually belongs to that period. In the 19th century many buildings were erected as virtual replicas of those of previous ages. They are often very beautiful and scholarly reproductions, and here, if they are to be distinguished from buildings of the periods they imitate, such factors as apparent age and the inherent probability of such a building existing at that place and time must be taken into account. This is often an easy matter, for more often than not the sham is very evident; but familiarity with the subject is sometimes necessary before a true estimate of date can be made. It has been said that for enjoyment of architecture a knowledge of dates is unimportant, and if pure aesthetic appreciation were the only benefit to be derived from a study of architecture this would be true. Archaeological interest, historical association, an understanding of structural problems and how they were overcome, all contribute to our enjoyment. Without some knowledge of dates this enjoyment would all be missed.

English architecture is an immense subject for so small a work, and in order to cover the ground it has been necessary to generalise, possibly at the expense of strict accuracy in some particulars. But the main story is clear and it is a story well worth learning, for it is a fact that architecture is the highest physical expression of man's endeavour, and in England there exists more beautiful architecture than in almost any country in the world.

Building Materials (see map on p. 167)

The subject of building materials is susceptible to no such chronological treatment as the other factors we have mentioned, for whereas skill and social needs change as time passes, and are more or less the same in all parts of the country at any one time, the materials available vary with locality, and change hardly at all with the passage of time. So some account of building materials, their uses and localities, must be given before coming to the main building story. Having once described these, no further specific reference will be made to local variations due to their influence.

In the days of bad communications, when a journey from London to Gloucester took three days if travelling light or nearly a week for heavy transport in good weather, clearly only the most expensive and elaborate buildings could afford to use any but local materials, and even then seldom for the main structure. Thus until the 18th and 19th centuries and the digging of canals and the laying of railways, local materials were all-important to local buildings. After this time cheap water transport inland, cheap coastwise traffic, and cheap railways enabled houses to be built often more economically in brick than in the local material. Churches and castles are the great exceptions to the general rule. The importance of religion and war to the medieval peoples was such that, if humanly possible, stone, the noblest and most lasting of their materials, would be transported for the work. Here water transport was used. The stone was quarried at a suitable coastal quarry and brought by ship round the coast and up the rivers until it could be shipped no further. After this it had to be carried over-land by packhorse.

The first and the most primitive building material is timber. Oak is the traditional English timber, all other woods that are useful structurally being foreigners, with the exception of elm, which is most usefully employed in connection with water, as in jetties, water-pipes, or as the outer sheathing to a building, like weather-boarding. At one time England was a densely forested land, the greater parts of the low-lying districts being

12

covered with oak woods. The 17th century saw the end of timber as the material for large houses. After this, timber had become too scarce owing to the inroads made in the forests by the charcoal burners and the farmers.

Subsequently only the smallest cottages in remote districts were built of oak. Later, in the 18th century, foreign softwood became available, especially in coastal areas of the south-east, and a temporary return to timber weather-boarding in sawn deal may be seen in districts that had a strong timber tradition. The principal districts for timber buildings are the Western Midlands (notably Worcestershire, Shropshire, Cheshire, and Lancashire), East Anglia, and Kent.

Building stones vary greatly from the hard granite of the west and north to the flints and chalk of East Anglia. But the best stone lies between these two extremes. This is the limestone that runs in a great belt across the country from Dorset through east Somerset, Gloucestershire, north Wiltshire, Oxfordshire, Northampton, Leicestershire, Nottinghamshire, to east Yorkshire. This limestone is one of the finest building stones in the world, and all along its track masons have taken advantage of its good weathering qualities, its ease of working, and its consistent texture, and a splendid building tradition has grown up wherever it occurs. This is perhaps most noticeable of all in the Cotswolds. Sandstones occur in the Midlands and in Yorkshire, but they are either hard and difficult to work or else they have comparatively poor weathering qualities and strength and are too friable. Chalk as a building stone was not used in the past, though recently experiments have been tried with some success. But chalk may be burnt for lime to make plaster, and in chalk there lie strata of flints. Brick and flint or stone and flint and much thick plasterwork may be expected in the chalk districts, the principal areas being east Dorset, Hampshire and Wiltshire, Salisbury Plain, the North and South Downs, and Kent, the Berkshire Downs, the Chilterns, Suffolk and Norfolk, and a small part of east Yorkshire. The hard rocks of the north and west, the millstone grit of the Pennines, and the granites of Wales and Cornwall are not easily worked and are very strong. Buildings in these areas tend to be very simple and rather crude.

The clay of the valley bottoms has since the time of the Romans been used for making bricks, but this material was not generally used until the 16th century, when timber was becoming scarce. Generally speaking, oak forests grow best on a clay subsoil, so from early times a combination of brick and timber was common, and later brick alone may be expected in most clay districts. East Anglia was the home of brick-making in medieval times, and still today more bricks are made in south-east England than anywhere else in the British Isles.

Social Conditions

Before starting a more detailed review of the Architecture of England, it is necessary to relate, in a very general way, the sequence of changing social conditions and the predominating building types that arose because of these conditions.

Broadly speaking, there are three main periods into which English architecture may be split: the Medieval, the Renaissance, and the Industrial.

The first, Medieval, covers a period during which men were influenced as never since by a tremendous religious preoccupation and fervour, and when life was very insecure.

The second, Renaissance, covers a period when intellect was considered all-important, religion had suffered a remarkable decline, and social organisation had advanced to a stage where a reasonable degree of security was assured.

The third, Industrial, period was that during which men were building for gain, when religion played an even smaller part in men's lives; and when England, after the defeat of Napoleon in the most expensive war she had fought, enjoyed a whole century of almost complete peace and a great measure of security for the individual.

Between these periods there came times of transition. One period slid either more or less rapidly into the next, the influences of the one greatly affecting the other, so that hard-and-fast boundaries of "period" become meaningless.

The Medieval period, which extended from the Dark Ages to the Reformation (about A.D. 600 to 1500), was far the longest of the three. During the whole of this time the buildings on which men lavished their greatest skill and care were those of a religious nature. The very fact that of all medieval buildings existing today, ninety-nine out of a hundred are either cathedrals, churches, or monasteries indicates that it was on this type of building that they spent most trouble and time, making them as enduring as they were able and incidentally sparing no pains to make them beautiful. The remainder are nearly all castles, which were built to subdue the country, to house the feudal lords, and to form part of a chain of defensive strong-points throughout the land. The internal wars, the necessity for the Norman invaders to govern the conquered Saxon by force, the bad blood that frequently existed between the Norman barons, and the general fear of foreign invasion all made the castle a necessity. Castles continued to be built on a more and more elaborate scale until the end of the 15th century, when the use of gunpowder had made them an anachronism, and the country was sufficiently secure internally to allow men to live without a constant fear that their neighbours might attack them.

At the beginning of this period, when the Saxons were newly converted to Christianity, the people were living a life of little security, and had very little skill in building in anything but timber. Their buildings have now nearly all disappeared except the crude stone churches, small and ill-lit, reflecting vividly the difficulties they had in overcoming the problems of what was to them an unusual building material. The constant invasions and threats of invasions gave them little inclination to undertake any very large-scale works and so they learnt better ways of building extremely slowly.

Although association with the Continent seems to have been fairly constant, they hardly benefited at all by the much greater skill of the Latin peoples. This is partly explained by the character of the Saxons. We are told in a contemporary French MS. that they lived very high, with much good food and drink, and loved songs and merrymaking, but that at the same time they lived in hovels. They were evidently a light-hearted, impractical, improvident people, utterly different from the more solemn and materialist Normans.

When the Normans occupied the land they brought their superior technical skill with them, and taught the Saxon how to build in the Norman manner. But since they had to use Saxon labour, semi-skilled by their standards, their buildings were at first very rough in finish, and their walls were built a good deal thicker than they need have been had they been able to cut their stones more accurately. As time passed building technique became more and more perfect, and one after another they solved their problems, until by the end of the 15th century a pitch of technical ability in masonry and carpentry was reached in England that has never been surpassed. All this time the great majority of buildings, that is the ordinary houses of the people, were in timber. What they were like in the early days we can only guess, for none have survived, but they were probably for the most part closely built clusters of single-storey, timber-framed houses, walled with woven osiers plastered with mud, and roofed with thatch. These houses were built under the shadow of the castles or huddled together inside their curtain walls for protection.

Each baron or local lord had his own following of retainers, who worked for him and fought for him, protected by his castle, which formed the nucleus of the community, isolated from neighbouring communities by leagues of forest and swamp. Later, when with the increase of population, prosperity, and trade this simple system became unwieldy, proper cities were formed. Most of the buildings were still in timber, except for the castles, churches, and monasteries, but there began to be formed a middle-class people, not rich enough to build a castle yet not of the unpaid servant class. These people built themselves farms and, when well-to-do, manor-houses. These were often of stone or brick.

The vast majority of buildings in this period then are ecclesiastical, with a number of castles that later give place to manor-houses. Although there are certain other sorts of buildings besides, these are the main types that dominate the Medieval era.

Towards the end of the Medieval period new influences of progressive political thought began to make themselves felt. The increase in the wool trade, and consequently in the prosperity of the country, brought about a system of land-renting for cash rather than for service, as had hitherto been the case. This was a very fundamental change, and resulted in the breakdown of the old feudal system and the rise to what was eventually to be freedom for the yeoman farmer and to a lesser degree of his paid servant. The Wars of the Roses saw the end of the feudal system. The great noble families that had hitherto held undisputed sway over the land ruined each other so completely that the yeoman farmers and gentlefolk now became the "upper class."

By Tudor times enough churches and cathedrals had been built to meet the needs of the people, and the final break between the Church and the Crown, always an uneasy team, resulted not only in the destruction of many monasteries but in an almost complete cessation of ecclesiastical building in favour of secular. Men now, during the Tudor age, had a greatly increased idea of material comforts. The wealth of the country was very much more evenly distributed than before and many country squires could afford to build themselves strong brick or oak houses. Cheap bricks had become universally popular. Even the king considered that it was a material suitable for his palaces. Gone was the time when only the greatest in the land could build in enduring stone, while the remainder built in mud and thatch; gone was the great church-building era. Domestic building in lasting materials had become possible for all but the poorest.

This, the beginning of the Renaissance in England, was a period of great mental and social upheavals. Not only was the omnipotence of Rome called in question and finally renounced in favour of new religious beliefs, but a deeper change which made such renunciation possible had come over the mentality of the people. This was a change from an unquestioning acceptance of the established order of social life and an un-questioning faith in the teachings of the Church, to an enquiring, experimenting attitude of mind that was a most adventurous departure from the well-known safe channels to which thought had hitherto been confined. This spirit of adventure encouraged enquiry on a rational and material basis, totally opposed to all previous beliefs. It is the spirit of reason which was the mainspring of all activities for the next two hundred years.

Under these circumstances material comforts and improvements in domestic building were natural, and the 17th and 18th centuries show a complete revolution in domestic architecture fol-lowed by a full development of the ordinary middle-class person's house, from the small medieval manor-house to the elegant, comfortable residence of the Georgian gentleman, a process greatly helped by the rapidly increasing wealth of the country.

One important and immediate result of the Renaissance was that learning was made possible for anyone who cared to acquire it, and was no longer confined to the monks and friars. A great number of colleges and schools were consequently founded in the Tudor period, and this class of building continued to be of some importance during succeeding centuries.

By the time of the 18th century the social order had again acquired a stability that seemed as permanent as the old feudal system. Wealth was concentrated once more into fewer hands and vast country estates were enclosed by wealthy men, to the exclusion of the small farmer. On these estates were built immense country homes of unparalleled grandeur. In the towns whole neighbourhoods were owned by single landowners, who were thus able to lay them out as residential building estates, making possible an organised town-planning of fine blocks of houses arranged in stately squares and crescents, a circumstance that would not have been possible had each inhabitant built and planned his own home as he had done in medieval times.

On the other hand land enclosure in the country and increased industrial activity in the coal and iron producing centres had resulted in the formation of new towns, towards which the dispossessed small-holder was inevitably drawn. During the 18th and 19th centuries, a prodigious increase in population took place; the reason for this is not certainly known. New homes had to be built for these people, and new factories sprang up everywhere, with their attendant interminable rows of depressing, cheap houses.

The last ten years of the 18th century and the first seventy-five of the 19th constitute a period of industrial development that proceeded at an almost frightening pace. This was made possible by the fact that coal and iron were available together in many parts of the country.

The industrial era cannot be said to have started at any particular date. Long ago in Tudor times machinery was in use for performing many of the processes in the manufacture of woollen cloth; and for the simpler tasks, such as grinding corn, machinery had been in existence for centuries before that. At first this was wooden machinery driven by water-power or wind-power. By this arrangement the workpeople were distributed over the length of the rivers that supplied the power, and not concentrated in towns. In 1712 a stationary steam-engine was invented and put to work pumping water from the mines in Cornwall. This machine was made partly of wood and was very simple and ponderous, but it marked a most important milestone in the development of the industrial revolution. The production of iron in bulk could not be achieved until a method was devised of using coal for smelting, for the universal fuel, wood, was fast disappearing. Late in the 18th century this difficulty was overcome, and iron became available in ever-increasing quantities to make machines for pumping-out the new deep coal-mines and for working the manufactories, to make bridges, railways, and finally, ships. From 1790 onwards the output of manufactured goods from the factories doubled and trebled every few years. The increase in goods traffic was enormous. At first elaborate canal systems were built; then railways were laid down. The first steam locomotive was in operation in 1804, a hundred years after the first steam-engine was used, and the first public railway was opened in 1825. Great engineering works in connection with transport were undertaken. Iron bridges, iron railway stations, tremendous tunnels, cuttings, and embankments, all were executed at a great pace.

Meanwhile the workpeople of the towns whence all the flood of manufactured articles originated were increasing and multiplying at a rate that exceeded the employment demand. Consequently labour was cheap, housing was bad, slums appalling, and profits vast.

Business increased with manufacture, so huge office blocks and banking-houses were needed, and the increased urban population made the invention of blocks of tenements and flats a necessity. Large shops and warehouses were built to deal with the ever-increasing flow of customers and goods; compulsory education was introduced and thousands of schools built; hospitals and public buildings of every sort were needed for the new towns and much "municipal" building was done.

The increasing efficiency of passenger transport gradually allowed more and more people to live outside the towns, and as the prosperity of the country grew so gradually the standard of living, which had dropped swiftly because of the increase in population, grew higher. In the late 19th and early 20th centuries these factors showed themselves in the growth of the suburban house. Although these small houses were a vast improvement on the crowded slums they helped to replace, they were mostly badly built, and since no organisation existed for town-planning they were almost invariably built in the wrong place. The necessity for a controlled planning of building activities on a national basis became more and more obvious as time passed, and gradually the old laws of property-ownership were modified to allow a greater measure of control to be exercised over the building activities of individuals. Now sufficient powers have been given to the authorities to permit a really efficient planning scheme that applies to both country and town to be realised.

We have now become familiar with such large nationally controlled building projects as the new towns, which have been described as a social experiment, as indeed they are. They might also be called a social necessity. Planning in its broadest sense is essential to control the further growth of existing towns and to prevent the chaotic spreadeagling of remoter and yet remoter suburbs, with all their attendant transport, educational and other social problems.

During the 19th century the principal types of buildings were industrial, commercial, and civic. In the 20th century the accent has been on domestic building and the improvement of public services, for today the demand is primarily for a higher standard of public health and education and for a more congenial environment for people to live in. Up to the end of the 18th century an ordered existence in England was possible. In the 19th century life became chaotic, for the increase in the speed of developments was much too sudden. It is the rectifying of the state of affairs which the industrial revolution brought about that is the chief concern of architects and planners today.

23

PART ONE

Buildings of the Medieval Period

CHAPTER I

PRE-CONQUEST OR SAXON
(600–1066)

SAXON CHURCHES are the oldest English buildings.
We are not concerned here with the buildings
of the Romans, visitors from
abroad, nor with the mysterious
works of the prehistoric peoples,
but with a more homely subject
—the parish church.

There are very few complete
Saxon churches left, but these
show clearly of what the in-
habitants of England in the Dark
Ages were capable when it came
to building.

Compared to the peoples of
later centuries the Saxons were
a primitive and uneducated folk,
but in the very earliest part of
the Saxon era, during the time
of the Venerable Bede, there
existed in the religious establish-

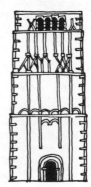

Saxon Tower

ments in England greater minds and a higher
culture than anything on the continent of
Europe. But this was not to last. Heathen

25

invasions from across the North Sea and internal wars played havoc with any possible progress, and the whole period is characterised by a series of more or less partial lapses into heathenism. During one of the longer periods of comparative stability, the country having become once again largely Christian, a considerable amount of church building was undertaken. It is from this period (600–800) that most Saxon churches probably date. Later, more heathens—Danes—invaded the country and destroyed many churches, and during the whole period of 800–1000 very little building appears to have been undertaken. It is not till the Norman conquest, or shortly before, that any real progress can be seen in building technique.

Of the few Saxon churches that remain, and churches are almost the only buildings that have lasted, all are small. They are the simplest possible sort of building, with the simplest possible windows and doors. The Saxons evidently had no idea of thinking of a church as anything more than a series of rooms joined together by narrow doorways. They built up their churches piecemeal like children playing with bricks. That the chancel and nave should be thought of as part of the same enclosed space had not occurred to them. They made the chancel arch so small and heavy that, whilst emphasising the shrine-like quality of

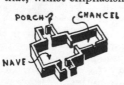

the chancel, they completely cut it off from the body of the church.

Although complete Saxon buildings are very rare, many churches have Saxon work in them, and

26

there are a number of smaller works such as stone crosses erected to mark the old crossings of ways. The Saxons were great tower-builders and it is this, the strongest part of the church, that has most often survived. Later enlargements of the structure have in many cases been made so long ago that it is often only by the details of the masonry that the earlier work may be distinguished. The exteriors of the churches were simple and were sometimes decorated with a criss-cross pattern, formed of long, thin stones let into the face of the rubble wall, that seems to have little meaning  or purpose. This decoration may be a derivation of Roman building forms, so debased as to be unrecognisable; or it may be derived from timber construction with which the Saxons were very familiar. The use of alternate vertical and horizontal stones at the corners, which is a debased form of the logical pattern made by any stone-mason who wants to make a strong corner to his building, is very typical of the awkward way in which the Saxons used stone, for timber was

Normal Corner Stones (L.) and Saxon Corner Stones (R.)

their natural traditional material, originating as they did from the forests of Northern Germany and Denmark.

Their windows and doors are like very small holes punched in very thick walls. Their windows are usually placed singly with round arches over them, or sometimes with only a simple triangle of stones instead of an arch. Where they ventured to make larger openings they used short pillars to

support the walls above. These were either plain shafts of stone or were crudely carved like balusters.

No roofs exist, for they have all long since disappeared, but there is a roof of a Saxon tower at Sompting, in Sussex, which is almost certainly original in shape.

The hall-mark of Saxon work is its crudeness and smallness; even their beautiful stone crosses are of simple bas-relief. When looking at Saxon work one feels more strongly than with that of any other period how remote and primitive the builders were.

CHAPTER II

NORMAN OR ROMANESQUE
(1066–1200)

NORMAN BUILDING has become a synonym for
solidity. What more rock-like and enduring than
the Norman castle keep? What more massive
than the vast cylinders of dressed stone that support the Norman church?

This was a new way of building introduced by
the foreigners, more ambitious and greater in size
and scope than anything the primitive Saxons had
been able to achieve.

Some big building in the French manner,
however, had been undertaken before the actual
landings by the Normans under William of Nor-
mandy in 1066, for communications with the
Continent had greatly improved. A much earlier
Westminster Abbey than the existing structure
was built before the Conquest, and a fine work it
must have been.

England was at last progressing, and she was
ripe for new ideas. What further progress she
would have made without the stimulus of the
Conquest and without the peace and security from
invasion that the powerful Norman military caste
lent her, it is difficult to say. Though slower,
architectural development must inevitably have
been on the same lines, but the next few hundred
years would not have been so coloured as they were
by French influence.

HEREFORD CATHEDRAL: EARLY 12TH CENTURY

After his decisive defeat of Harold at Hastings, Duke William set about subduing and organising the country in the most businesslike manner. He brought with him his court, his lords, and his barons. He brought his highly organised and zealous churchmen, and he brought his soldiers, his common people. The social system that existed in England was as well suited to a military dictatorship as it was to a more peaceful way of life, and he modified it but little. Under this system the unpaid serf gave his work and his service to his master in return for the protection and security that his master's organised household could afford him; the household organised for defence and for agriculture. The freed man who was in a position to employ unpaid serfs would receive his land from his next social superior, and would pay rent to him in the form of men-at-arms on demand in case of need. The small barons rented their land from the great barons on the same basis, and they in their turn were granted manors, or large tracts of land, from the king, who would demand a very considerable payment for his grant. This, the feudal system, was ideal for a population made up of isolated communities, organised on a military basis, and all owing allegiance to one king.

William's first task was to make the country secure, and to do this he granted his barons permission to build castles on their manors, strongholds to overawe the Saxons by their magnitude and to serve as strongpoints in case of rebellion. As a temporary measure the barons built themselves wooden castles, later replacing them by huge stone keeps which they used not only to maintain order within their own domains and to house themselves and their garrison, but also as bases from which to harass the neighbouring barons, in order to secure more land for themselves.

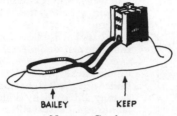

BAILEY   KEEP

Norman Castle

The second of William's great tasks was to establish his church. He and his people were ardent Christians, and after the initial period of warfare had ceased, during which no church building took place, a very great number of parish churches, cathedrals, abbeys, and monasteries were built. The cathedrals were to be the largest buildings ever seen in this country, buildings that must have amazed the Saxons, who, of course, had to do most of the work.

Norman Church

Thus, early in the Norman period, social and therefore building activities split naturally into two divisions—secular and religious. The secular buildings, after the initial castle-building era, became relatively unimportant. The religious buildings continued to gain in importance and size until the Reformation.

The main characteristic of all Norman work is its massiveness and its roundness: round arches,  massive cylindrical columns, thick flat walls, and sometimes round buildings altogether like the Temple Church in London or the chapel at Ludlow Castle. To the Norman designer the square and the circle were the most important shapes. The Normans built with small stones, and using, as they did, partially skilled Saxon labour, their early walls and pillars were very crudely built. Their method was to rely on the dead weight and solidity of their walls to take the sideways thrusts of the arches. They used only a few shallow buttresses, mere thickenings of the walls, to take the added loads at special points. They cut as few stones as they could, making their walls and pillars of two skins of cut stones and filling in the space inside with rubble. This method is not so strong as building

with larger and properly fitted stones, so they had to make their walls and piers much thicker than they would otherwise have needed to do, which in its turn increased the weight that had to be supported—a vicious circle. Small wonder that their pillars look so thick and massive.

This method was most unsatisfactory and cases are known where a whole tower fell down almost as soon as it was built. This happened at Winchester Cathedral. The Normans frequently used no scaffolding, long, straight timbers being hard to come by. Some idea may be gained of the tremendous amount of labour they were prepared to spend on their buildings from the fact that in building this tower at Winchester they constructed a ramp of earth, it is said, on which to carry their stones to the top. After the building was finished they would have had to dig all the earth away again, a task which in itself, with the primitive tools available, must have drained the labour resources of half the county.

These towers were squat and square, lending to all Norman churches and cathedrals a stocky

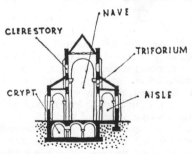

appearance that is unmistakable. In the bigger churches and cathedrals the pillars, thick and round, supported semi-circular arches to hold the high walls of the clerestory above. The space made by the aisle roofs was sometimes used for another small arcade of arches, the triforium, which made a passage-way round the building at a high level and helped to lighten the heavy wall.

Perhaps the most interesting feature of Norman buildings is the roof. Usually they roofed their

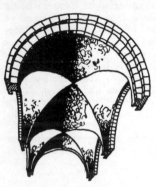

buildings with timber, boarding in the roof-trusses to make a tunnel-shaped ceiling, but from the earliest stages they put stone-vaulted roofs to their underground crypts, where it was easy to construct in the heavier material at ground level. Later, they made stone roofs for the main parts of the building too, partly because they wanted their important buildings to be as durable as possible, for the risk of fire to a wooden roof was very real. Except in Ireland, where an entirely different sort of roof was invented, the roof was not altogether of stone. They built a stone inner-vault and put a steep wooden roof on top of it.

The development of the stone inner-vault is so important that it is given here in detail. Not only is it intrinsically interesting but it illustrates most aptly that structural necessity and practical requirements were the cause of the introduction of features in a building that give it its "style," and that style was by no means a pleasing way of building which the builders used because they thought it "looked nice." At the same time a preconceived idea of what a building should be, before ways and means of making it so are discussed, is bound to influence the general shape of a building. For instance, the powerful but almost unconscious desire for their churches to aspire and to have a sense of mystic magnificence and reaching for the heavens, undoubtedly made the Medieval church-builders want to build as high as they dared and want to make their roofs look as light and delicate as possible. It is from these basic desires that the method of construction largely springs, and from the necessities of the construction that those shapes arise that people so often think of as the hall-marks of a "style." The true hall-mark of a period is the shape, the proportion, and the method of construction and details all thought of as a whole, and all arising from the basic idea behind the building. This idea was itself absolutely governed by the lives and thoughts of the people of the time, by their needs and aspirations, by their way of looking at things, and the ratio in which they held some things to be more important than others. It is only by a careful study of the peoples' lives and thoughts that a real understanding of architecture may be derived. However, the scope of this book is not wide enough to allow of any very detailed account of these matters, but because no further stress is laid on this aspect of architecture it is not to be thought that it is unimportant.

The most elementary sort of vault known to the Normans was the Barrel vault, which was

37

simply a tunnel; by making two barrel vaults intersect at right-angles, a groined cross-vault was

achieved. This was built solidly of thick masonry, requiring a very strong wooden frame to hold the stones in place while it was being built, and makes a

roof to the square intersection of two equally wide passageways. If, however, a vaulted roof to an arcade of arches is required, it is possible to repeat the central motif alone and omit the "barrels." This the Normans did, usually in their crypts.

In order, however, to lessen the amount of timber centering, as the temporary support is called, they found it convenient to build proper arches between the columns first, and build the groined vault between them afterwards. This was the most usual way of building a groined vault. But the vault was not, even so, very strong. The junction between the two original barrels along the groins was always weak. In attempting to overcome this difficulty and in attempting to make the shape of their roofs more definite and pleasing to the eye, they hit upon the plan of making diagonal arches first, quite separately, as

38

self-supporting members, and filling in between the diagonal and side arches with comparatively thin panels of stone work. This is a much stronger roof and an easier one to make, but as

soon as it was tried the question arose of what was the best shape for the diagonal arches to take. As the diagonal ribs were to be semi-circular arches, then the top of the vault would be a great deal higher in the centre than at the sides, producing a series of inverted saucers. This was not a popular solution to the problem in this country, and it was solved at first by making the diagonal a much flatter arch, i.e. segmental, not semi-circular. This looks awkward and does not carry the vertical line of the column smoothly into the roof. Peterborough Cathedral aisles are an example. All these vaults, however, were only suitable for roofing over squares. If the plan demanded an oblong shape, the arches along the long sides became much higher than those along the short sides. At first the builders found a way round this in starting the arches across the short sides very much higher up than the top of the column from which they sprang. These stilted arches looked very queer and unsatisfactory, and provided a poor abutment for any neighbouring arches that sprang from the capitals in the ordinary way. We may imagine with what misgivings the man who first thought of using a pointed arch tried the experiment.

But a pointed arch was to be the solution to all the difficulties. Not only could its amount of pointedness be varied without jarring on the eye, allowing unequal spans to be the same height at the top, but it allowed the big diagonal rib to spring vertically from the capital in a strong true sweep that continued upwards the even flow of the columns and carried the eye straight to the highest point of the building. From this stage vaulting problems were easily overcome. Now it was merely a matter of refinement.

The pointed arch was invented and used in Durham Cathedral as early as 1130, but did not come into general use till the end of the century.

Norman windows and doors were small, round-headed openings in thick walls. Often if they wanted a simple rectangular door they filled in the arch with a large, semi-circular stone called a tympanum.

This they decorated with spirited carvings which were of a character that is easily recognised. Lively and often humorous, the Norman carver had a technique that is inimitable. He seldom attempted anything other than low relief and his subjects though ostensibly religious, were, when he carved a scene with people in it, frankly secular in feeling. Mythological beasts, horsemen, soldiers, bishops, children—all were

shown with a delightful simplicity and directness of carving, due largely to the limitations of the carver's tools and skill. The secular carvings show to what extent religion was mixed with everyday. Simple abstract patterns mixed with stiff, formal foliage were much used, often in early work based on intertwining basket-work designs of Celtic origin. The arches over their windows and doors, more particularly over the latter, often consisted not of one thick arch but of a series of concentric rings of arches, receding into the thickness of the wall. These were normally carved, each ring of stones with a different pattern, and each stone being carved as one whole section of a repeating motif, irrespective of its size. This gave a slightly irregular quality to their carving which, although unintentional, is extremely pleasing to the eye. Some doors have as many as six or seven columns each side, supporting six or seven arches. The capitals of the Norman columns are often elaborately carved with

beasts and stiff formal foliage, but the most usual capital consists of a large flat square stone, or abacus, on which to build the arch spring, and beneath it a deep "cushion cap" which changes the square shape of the arch spring into the round shape of the column. On very thick columns the typical scalloped pattern that this change of shape suggested was repeated many times, and the abacus was sometimes made in the form of an octagon. In

the more highly decorated buildings the shafts of the columns were carved with big zigzags and spirals. The feet of the columns were normally very simply treated, with a wider course of stones at the bottom to spread the weight, carved into a round-shaped moulding, sitting on a square of masonry. Sometimes the corners of the square were covered over with a leaf to make them look more finished.

The Norman staircase that was used in both church and castle was of the ordinary spiral sort with a vertical central shaft, each step being built into the wall at one end and leaving a round lump at the other which became the shaft. This sort of staircase was universal and was the only sort of stone stair in general use in this country for hundreds of years.

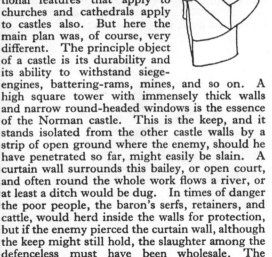

All the details and constructional features that apply to churches and cathedrals apply to castles also. But here the main plan was, of course, very different. The principle object of a castle is its durability and its ability to withstand siege-engines, battering-rams, mines, and so on. A high square tower with immensely thick walls and narrow round-headed windows is the essence of the Norman castle. This is the keep, and it stands isolated from the other castle walls by a strip of open ground where the enemy, should he have penetrated so far, might easily be slain. A curtain wall surrounds this bailey, or open court, and often round the whole work flows a river, or at least a ditch would be dug. In times of danger the poor people, the baron's serfs, retainers, and cattle, would herd inside the walls for protection, but if the enemy pierced the curtain wall, although the keep might still hold, the slaughter among the defenceless must have been wholesale. The living-quarters of the baron himself were in the keep, and a cheerless, comfortless place it must have been. No glass in the windows—only oak shutters to temper the icy winds—rushes on the stone floor, and the smoke from the roaring fire escaping where it might through windows and roof, blackening the stone walls and ruining the tapestries that were carefully stitched by the womenfolk to make the place a little less grim, for it was only the most palatial keeps that had the luxurious fireplace, a round-arched recess with a crude flue that led through the outside wall.

It is on this note of uncompromising grimness that we leave the Normans, and we will see how the forthright square-and-circle thinking of this period slides into the more highly developed and sophisticated austerity of the next.

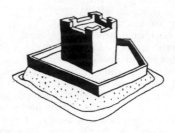

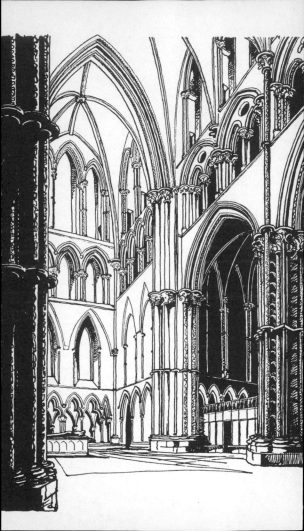

CHAPTER III

THE EARLY ENGLISH PERIOD
(1201–1300)

THIS IS the earliest phase of the style known as Gothic. Gothic was a term of derision, implying barbarity, given to Medieval architecture by the classicists of the 18th century. It is difficult to imagine a more inappropriate word with which to describe the great engineering feats that were the cathedrals of the 13th and 14th centuries. But the name has stuck, and having lost all its original meaning is now used quite without any intention of disparagement.

The Early English style of building covers that period when England was becoming more settled, when the distinction between Norman and Saxon was becoming less marked, and when the complete autocracy of the sovereign was smashed by a community of nobles, who must already have felt themselves to be English.

The Crusades of the 12th century had enabled the Normans to learn much of Eastern architecture, particularly of Eastern military engineering, in which the Saracens excelled. Intercourse with the continent of Europe was constant, and new ideas developed there were immediately used at home. It was during this period that the high ideology of the Church became fully developed. The intense desire for salvation in the next world,

---

LINCOLN CATHEDRAL, SOUTH-WEST TRANSEPT,
13TH CENTURY

coupled with an awful fear of damnation, gave rise to a preoccupation with life after death that had probably not been equalled in the world since the days of Ancient Egypt. All actions were coloured by their imagined effect on chances of salvation, and Heaven and Hell were no mere figures of speech but very real places for one of which all mankind was inevitably bound.

Outside the body of the Church no one could write or read, so medieval builders symbolised their religious beliefs in wood and stone, making their churches and cathedrals dramatised representations of their ideals, and incorporating in

Early English Cathedral

them such incidental and picturesque stories from the Bible as could be rendered in carving and stained-glass. The Early English builders made their churches as austere as possible, a symbol of the renunciation of the flesh and of worldly riches. They built their cathedrals as high as they dared, a symbol of man reaching to heaven; a church that would stand head-and-shoulders

48

above the surrounding landscape, dominating the wretched hovels that men lived in, a symbol of the power and strength of their faith soaring above the poor earthly creatures at its foot and showing a promise of the mystic majesty of the life to come. From such inspiration came the dark, tall cathedrals and the austere and simple parish churches of the 13th century.

Early English Parish Church

The greater security of the country and the better organisation of the Church led the clergy to seek finer ceremonial to grace their services. This was in itself an incentive to great church building in order to make possible the full beauty of their ritual.

The large amounts with which the monasteries were endowed enabled ecclesiastical buildings to be undertaken on an ever-increasing scale. The Church at this time owned as much as one-fifth of the land, and the importance of the monastic establishments can hardly be over-emphasised. Quite apart from being the centres that fostered the all-pervading influence of religious thought, the monasteries had almost the entire monopoly of learning. Such knowledge of medicine as existed, the most up-to-date theories of agriculture, and, above all, the science of architecture

4   49

were all the exclusive property of the monasteries. No major development in the structural principles of medieval building, with the possible exception of the timber roof, was due to any but their influence.

A large monastery consisted essentially of the monastic church, the cloister, the chapter house,

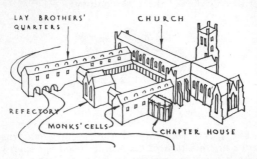

The Monastery

the sacristy and the living quarters of the monks. After the dissolution of the monasteries, the monastic church often became a cathedral. The living quarters consisted of the dormitory, the refectory, and the kitchens. The dormitory frequently adjoined the church and, in the establishments of certain orders, consisted of a series of cells. The chapter house often consisted of a separate building, a polygonal vaulted chamber of great beauty, in which the business of the establishment, both secular and spiritual, was transacted. The dissolution of the monasteries in the time of Henry VIII was so wholesale that none now exist except in a ruined condition.

Engineering skill had greatly increased during the last 50 years, and builders had come to a proper understanding of the thrusts set up inside a structure based on arches. Stone cutting was by now improved out of all recognition, so that, although churches were built much taller than before, their supports could become more slender and the whole structure very much lighter. Pillars were now built in solid dressed stones all fitting tightly together and able to bear greatly increased weights, but most walls were still built with rubble cores as before.

The structural principle of the Early English church is that walls are only built thick enough to withstand the sideways pushing of the arches at those points where the arches join them. Be-tween these points, the wall may be as thin as practicable. This means that if the roofing and vaulting thrusts come between the windows, there the wall is made immensely thick. The thickening of the wall had to be so deep that it became, in fact, a short cross wall that took the thrust along its length. But this sort of buttress is only adequate to take the thrusts of arches that spring immediately from it. The lighting of large churches and cathedrals complicated the issue, for with so wide a building it is necessary to have more light than could be admitted through side

windows only, or the centre of the building would
remain dark. So the centre of all big churches
is raised up and clerestory windows are put in.
The thrust of the vault of the main roof, however,

has now to be somehow transferred across the
aisle roof to the supporting buttresses. An arch
flung across the gap at an angle was found to be
the solution. These flying buttresses, which
may be compared to the familiar timber shoring
seen supporting many buildings when under
reconstruction, take the weight of the nave roof
and vaulting, and pass it downwards and outwards
to the great buttresses on the outer wall. In
the nave of Westminster Abbey (1245–1270) where
the cloister joins on to the aisle, the whole thing
had to be taken a stage further and double flying
buttresses were incorporated, taking the thrusts
of the new ribbed vaults right out over the double
distance in two stages. The pinnacles were put
on top of the thin buttress walls to give them
added weight. As each flying buttress puts its
weight on to the main buttress, so the main
buttress becomes correspondingly thicker to take
the added strain, the thickenings being sloped
off to shed the rainwater. In small buildings

the buttresses were shallower because the load was less.

All this was pure engineering, and all with one end in view, that of obtaining as high a building

with as economical a use of stone as possible. The builders in no way attempted to hide their methods of construction, they made no attempt to conceal their flying buttresses. In the case of Westminster Abbey the whole exterior is practically undecorated; it is a simple, straightforward expression of an engineering feat in dressed stone. The 13th-century designers never had any doubts about using bold simple forms in their buildings, expressing simply in stone what their buildings were and how they were made. The results were

powerful and moving designs.

The characteristic features of this period are the form of the arch, which has now become pointed, the tall thin windows, and the general accent on height and verticality, and all the structural features arising from this.

No definite distinction can be made between one period and another, and the gradual change from what was typically Norman to what was typically Early English is as much an architectural "period" as the periods themselves, which have been used for convenience and are not watertight compartments dividing one sort of building rigidly from another. As already described, the pointed arch and the ribbed vault had been discovered during the Norman period. The first experiments were made somewhere about 1130, and these were to bear full fruit during the next century. Often Norman walls were decorated by

a bas-relief pattern of intersecting arches. Although the pointed arch was a structural necessity, not only because it was the means of overcoming the vaulting problems described in the last chapter but be-

cause it was far stronger than the round arch and exerted far less lateral thrust, it is by no means impossible that the first idea of a pointed arch was derived from this pattern.

The pointed arch is exclusively used in the vaulting of this period. No fundamental structural changes came about in vaulting, the Early English being merely an elaboration of the Norman system. Additional ribs were introduced between the main cross ribs and the diagonals, which, whilst allowing the panels between the ribs to become lighter, necessitated the introduction of further ribs along the ridges of the vaults against which the intermediates could lean.

Another interesting feature of the change from Norman to Early English was the use of the chisel, superseding the old axe for stone carving. Previously all carving, though often barbaric in its richness, had been in very low relief, clinging

Early Norman—Late Norman

closely to the member it adorned. Now, with the introduction of the chisel, considerable undercutting was possible, and it is fascinating to see how the later 12th-century stone-carver loved to undercut with this new tool and how he made the formal clinging patterns cut by his predecessors sprout from the stone. In its fully developed Early English form the decoration

Early English

of the capitals became a deeply undercut, very formalised pattern of leaves, with a strong feeling of supporting what was above it. Great strength of contrasting dark shadow with high-lit stone was the outcome of this undercutting, and when

applied to mouldings round an arch, very powerful and dramatic such details can be. This deeply cut moulding was also used for capitals where foliage was not employed. No longer were the simple zigzags and geometrical shapes used as they had been. The old zigzag, by

56

increased undercutting, became a pattern known as dogtooth, a series of completely hollowed pyramids, used sparingly now on a few features of the building that the designer wanted to look particularly rich.

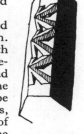

A startling change too had come about in window design. Towards the end of the 12th century glass for windows became available, and life had become more settled so that the church was less likely to be used as a place of refuge. This, together with the advantage of the windows occurring in the thin wall between the buttresses, enabled the builders to make their windows much larger. The typical early window of the period was tall and thin, with the new pointed arch at its head like a lancet. Soon groups of lancets were arranged together between pairs of buttresses. The desirability of making some sort of hood to prevent driving rain from running down the face of the building into the window was realised, and this gave the builders

the idea of coupling the groups of windows together, and finally of punching holes through the

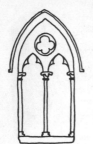

blank spaces left between the hood moulding and the lancets. This is called Plate Tracery, and in its later stages it was further elaborated into trefoils and quatrefoils. This style of Early English architecture is sometimes called "Geometric Style."

The Norman pillars of the last century were made of rubble with dressed stone faces. Now columns were made with solid blocks and were decorated with completely detached shafts of polished limestone or Purbeck Marble. These shafts were supported with small bonding stones that make the characteristic "rings" seen at intervals up their length. In the later stages of this period the shafts were to become merged with the parent column to form a multiple column that further increased the verticality of the design.

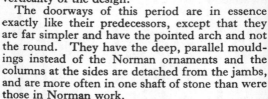

The doorways of this period are in essence exactly like their predecessors, except that they are far simpler and have the pointed arch and not the round. They have the deep, parallel mouldings instead of the Norman ornaments and the columns at the sides are detached from the jambs, and are more often in one shaft of stone than were those in Norman work.

The Early English builders were very fond of detaching shafts from their background, and it is

58

one of the chief characteristics of their work. This increased desire to have their details free-standing is evidence of an increased interest in space. They were no longer, as the Normans were, so interested in mass, but liked to create a feeling of spaciousness by allowing the eye to travel past objects in the immediate foreground and glimpse possibilities of further spaces beyond.

The castles of the period were very much more elaborate than the simple Norman keep. Halls,

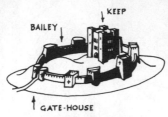

13th Century Castle

for a degree of comfort that was impossible in the keep, were built within the walled ring, or, if none existed, walls were built. These were not always built concentrically as those shown in the diagram, for often the keep itself formed too valuable a redoubt to be buried inside the works. In this case the wall would be taken up to each side of the keep, which then became the principle tower in the wall. Crenellation and all the intriguing features of medieval military architecture, like shoots, down which to pour molten lead or boiling pitch, portcullises and drawbridges—all were invented towards the close of this period.

CHAPTER IV

THE DECORATED PERIOD
(1301–1400)

In the 14th century the simplicity and economy of Early English building gave place to a more highly decorated style. No longer were church builders content to make an unadorned pinnacle or spire without decorating it with knobs and crockets of stone; the simple, narrow windows of the preceding century now became a riot of colour and curved tracery. Buildings generally became more profuse in decoration, better lit, and more lavish in their proportions. The accent was all

14th Century Cathedral

on gaiety and elaboration. Glass had by now become far less of a rarity, and the highly decorative coats-of-arms, crests and blazons of the nobility, no less than the greater light-heartedness of the buildings, express the increased happiness of the country, for England was rapidly becoming

TINTERN ABBEY: EARLY 14TH CENTURY

a prosperous nation, and with prosperity came an increased love of gaiety and comfort.

Domestic buildings, other than those of a purely military character, had become more common as the homes of a growing class of reasonably wealthy yeomen. This was also a great period of improvement and enlargement of the parish church. The

Decorated Parish Church

gloomy little churches of the previous century with their narrow windows and shed-like aisles and lack of clerestory lighting, no longer fulfilled the more exacting needs of the people, who wanted light and cheerfulness in their religion as in their lives. The castle was by now as impregnable as it was ever to be, surrounded by high, towered curtain walls defying the trebuchet, or two-ton catapult, and the sapper alike. The new plate-armour was succeeding the old chain-mail and military sports such as the tournament were popular. All was gay and colourful, human and brave, just as Chaucer described it. The code of secular integrity and honour that had been formulated among the knights and nobles was of an astonishingly high order. The Knights' ideals of chivalry were very fine, however far short of them they may have come in practice, and are evidence

of a highly organised and delicately balanced
society.

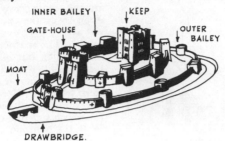

A Late Castle

The second half of the century is overshadowed
by the calamity of the Black Death (1348–49),
after which very little big building was done.
However, a larger measure of independence was
gained by the hitherto unpaid labourer class, for
labour was in short supply after the plague, a
factor which gave the serfs an advantage over their
employers. The discontent following on the
attempts of the landlords to rectify the inevitable
inflationary tendencies that the labour shortage
brought about was a contributory cause to the
lack of building activity.

Manor-houses became of some importance
during this century. Although there are few
examples left, and even fewer of those of preceding
periods, the development of the house is of considerable importance. The nucleus of the
medieval house was the hall, and round this
nucleus the house-plan continued to develop
until the Renaissance. Houses in early Saxon

63

times were single-unit wooden buildings consisting of a roof supported on wooden posts and walls.

A Saxon House

In the centre was an open fire, the smoke escaping where it might. The aristocracy had similar, but better built halls. Round the fire the servants ate and slept, whilst the lord of the house occupied a raised dais at one end. With the Norman conquest the hall idea was not abandoned, the castle keep incorporating a precisely similar hall on the first floor. By the 13th century conditions had become more secure and the fortified manor-house was a practicable proposition. This was a development of the original Saxon hall, but with various improvements. Built in stone or brick with a timber roof, the house now consisted of a large room, open to the roof, with the same open fire. This was the hall in which the servants and retainers lived; at one end was the solar, or private room, for the lord of the manor and his family, a room usually on the first floor leading off the raised dais where he had his meals, and at the other end were the kitchens, separated from the hall by screens. The entrance was at the side, at the kitchen end, and beneath the solar was a storeroom. The classic example of this typical arrangement is the hall of the Castle of Stokesay, in Shropshire. By the 14th century further improvements and additions had been made. The manor-house now consisted of the main hall, still open to the roof, divided from the kitchens by a buttery, over which was a guest room. The entrance was elaborated into a porch over which a gallery for musicians was sometimes built. As

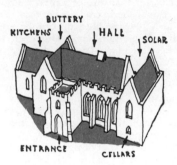

14th Century Manor-House

yet the various elements—the hall, the kitchens, and the solar—are roofed over separately, the solar and buttery or kitchen roofs running at right angles to the main roof of the great hall.

Bricks were used almost for the first time since the days of the Romans. They made their appearance in East Anglia, where contact was closest with the Netherlands, whence the bricks came. Foreign innovation as they were, bricks were used only in secular buildings and in this century only in a few isolated examples. The great flood of popularity for bricks was not to come for a long time. The normal building material for any wealthy building was still stone, and not for many years were the common people able to build in anything but the most perishable materials. The small domestic buildings that have lasted from this century are those of the rich merchants or well-to-do farmers, people of small account when compared with the great barons, but richer by far than the peasants. Towns were by now established trading-centres and permanent town houses, both of timber and stone, were built in large numbers. However, few have survived because of destruction by fire, and because the more rapidly changing economic conditions that exist in towns make the townsman a keen moderniser compared to his more conservative country cousin.

The principal contribution of the 14th century to the ecclesiastical architecture of this country was the development of the window. No startling change came over the design of buildings as a whole, no new structural principles were evolved. It is a period of development rather than invention. The increase in availability of glass, together with the new fashion of using imported coloured glass in the windows, assisted the designer to a conception of the window on a scale of size and beauty yet unknown.

The early Norman window had sometimes consisted of two openings linked with one arch. In the next century we have seen how the Early

Decorated Cathedral

66

English builders continued this idea, by introducing plate tracery by piercing the blank wall enclosed above the openings with simple circular or quatrefoil holes.

In the 14th century this develops into true window tracery, based on simple geometrical forms, consisting of curved bars of stone all supported on vertical bars or mullions, and retaining

the mullion shape in section throughout. The elaboration of small arches and pierced shapes into trefoils and quatrefoils followed.

From this geometrical basis where pointed arches and circles are the only motifs used, the

ogee—convex and concave—arch was evolved. This is a 14th-century invention and is the basis of most curvilinear tracery. Once freed from the rigid plain shapes of the so-called geometrical tracery, the early 14th-century masons lavished

their skill on a riot of curved stonework, employing free, fantastic shapes of great beauty.

However, the uncouth shapes that were often found inevitable where the arch cut the tracery cannot have pleased the designers, and we shall see what effect this had on the window design of the next century.

The method of allotting centuries to architectural periods must not be taken too literally. They are the centuries during which the bulk of the typical work of the periods was carried out, but many country districts were years behind the times and many a cathedral was half a century ahead. Thus in 1340 the choir at Gloucester was being built in the Perpendicular style, well ahead of its time, while in remote districts, particularly where there was a strong local building tradition, the Early English methods were still in force.

Early English vaulting developed in the Decorated Period only in its greater technical efficiency. The panels between the ribs were made lighter and the number of ribs was further increased, even to the extent of building short ribs spanning from the main ribs, forming star-like geometrical patterns on the roof that did not help in the construction of the panels in between. The many rib junctions were decorated with stone knobs or bosses, elaborately carved with faces, grotesques, and naturalistic foliage. The fine stylish carving of the 13th century developed into

a much more elaborate technique, the carver often trying to make in stone exact replicas of natural foliage, with a consequent great loss of beauty and fitness of form. Indeed the excellence of the craftsmanship of this period was allowed to get quite out of hand, resulting in tremendous over-elaboration of carved work. The smaller and more highly decorated parts of buildings, such as tombs and monuments, are frequently smothered beneath growths of stony foliage of a tropical luxuriance, and the vaulting bosses look more like huge cabbages and cauliflowers stuck on the ceiling rather than carved pieces of stone. The

same decadence in design is noticeable in the capitals of columns, where the foliage no longer has the feeling of simple strength and the supporting quality of Early English work.

Columns are taller and still more slender than those of the Early English period,

better built, and with no free standing shafts.
These shafts have now become joined to the parent
body of the column to make a cluster of piers, while

14 TH CENTURY

13 TH CENTURY

the mouldings round the arches are far less deeply
cut and a general flattening out of detail and design
is noticeable. The definite and startling contrasts
that were necessary in the gloom of Early English
buildings had become redundant and over-accen-
tuated in the better-lit interiors of the 14th century.

Castles of this date are comparatively rare, but
many older castles were enlarged and elaborated.
High, many-towered curtain walls, outer defences,
barbicans, and crenellations were added to older
buildings. By this time the keep had been largely
abandoned as the principal living-place of the
owner, and was relegated to the comparatively
unimportant role of the prison, storehouse, and
arsenal. Indeed, the military role of the castle
was fast declining and the nobles were building
huge vaulted halls within their towered baileys,
elaborate suites of stone rooms on a scale impossible to confine within the narrow limits of a
fortress keep. The castle extends outwards in a
complicated series of inner and outer wards,

70

courtyards and rings of walls, towered and em-battled. One is tempted to surmise that the technique of military engineering had already far outrun its uses, a state of affairs that was more marked in the next century, when castles were erected for effect and show, indeed, almost for fun.

CHAPTER V

THE PERPENDICULAR PERIOD
(1401–1500)

THE KEYNOTE of Perpendicular design is that of sophisticated restraint, coupled with a mechanical precision of detailing and proportion that seems to lend to the masonry a quality almost metallic. Walls are finished so fine as to seem infinitely thin,

while the windows are so large that the building is more like a huge glass box held up by fine shafts of stone than one of stone walls with windows pierced in them.

We have seen how during the preceding centuries the efficiency of building methods has steadily improved, growing from the crude beginnings to a great degree of technical perfection.

KING'S COLLEGE, CAMBRIDGE, THE CHAPEL: LATE
15TH CENTURY

We have seen also how from the aesthetic standpoint stone carving and the general elaboration of form have degenerated, and how the too-skilful mason has allowed his chisel to run away with him.

What is to be expected next? Clearly, either a further elaboration of what was tending already to become over-elaborate or something entirely new.

Up to this time all the building styles in England had had their counterparts on the Continent, particularly in France. Although not always exactly contemporary, the developments of architecture in the two countries had been very closely united.

Perpendicular Cathedral

It is now, at this last stage of Gothic building, that English builders strike out for the first time on a line of their own. In France the last stages of Gothic developed into a style known as Flamboyant, all curves and carving. But in England a return to comparative simplicity and austerity of design took place. Why this should have been is not certain.

It has been said that the shortage of craftsmen due to the Black Death made for simplification in design, as the former building methods were too difficult. This, even if it be true, can only be a small part of the solution. Some of the earlier

74

works were designed and built in the Perpendicular manner before the Black Death, and after the epidemic was over hardly any building was undertaken for some time. After the enforced pause, the new style emerges practically in its only and fully fledged form.

One immediate effect of the Black Death was the growth of the change in the farms from arable to pasturage for sheep, as a measure for saving labour. The wool trade was soon booming and a tremendous increase in trade, marketing, and transport took place. Bridges and town halls, market places and inns were by now being built in great numbers. Yeomen farmers made their fortunes, and many men who had been tied to the land as virtual slaves before were now building their own manor-houses. Although the emancipation of the serfs was not yet complete it was nearly so. Great numbers of parish churches were built and additions to many cathedrals were carried out with the money made from wool.

15th-century Market Cross

The art of printing (1477) aided the stimulus

Perpendicular Parish Church

that had been given to the founding of colleges and schools, many of which were built during this period.

Castles were no longer able to withstand sieges. Gunpowder had by now come into such general use in warfare as to alter completely the conception of investing tactics. Consequently houses designed as non-defensive homes were now built in large numbers for the first time, such magnificent places as Bodiam, Hurstmonceaux, and Warwick being among the last of the genuine castles built for defensive purposes. But even these were built very largely for show.

The manor-house continued to develop. Extra accommodation for guests and servants—for travel was becoming an easier matter—was provided by building extra suites of rooms and out-buildings in the form of a courtyard in front of the entrance door of the hall. The hall was still used as before, the open fire place still sending its smoke up to the open beams of the roof. The importance of the dais at the end of the hall was often accentuated by a larger window that reached to the floor. Big windows of this nature had to face into the courtyard, which was defended by a gate house, for although the country was becoming more secure, a measure of defence was still maintained. Oriel windows were often used in the solar and more important upper-floor rooms, such as that over the buttery. This was a new invention, a bay window, rectangular or half-octagonal in shape, that stuck out at first-floor level. The solar was now provided with a fireplace, and the walls of the upper chambers were even panelled in oak, a great improvement on the cold stone walls of the previous centuries.

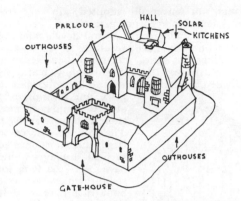

PARLOUR | HALL | SOLAR | KITCHENS | OUTHOUSES | OUTHOUSES | GATE-HOUSE

15th-Century Manor-House

As regards the detailed appearance of Perpendicular buildings the most noticeable distinguishing features are the lower and flatter arch, which appears in most work, the simplification of window tracery, which is universal, and the beautiful development of rib-vaulting into its last and most highly advanced stage, fan vaulting, which is seen only in the most expensive work of the period.

As a means of spanning over a space with the smallest rise in height, the four-centred arch was evolved. This and its variations,

77

although not universally adopted, are very frequently found in Perpendicular work.

In church building the natural development of the structure continued, resulting in larger windows filling the entire wall space between even deeper buttresses. The large windows had to be subdivided by stone members to keep the glass in

place, and a simple grid of vertical and horizontal stone bars was evolved. The windows were so large that unconnected vertical mullions would have been too long for stability unless they were built disproportionately thick. Where the main arch springs, the bars branch out into simple tracery, the vertical members of the grid usually being continued through the pattern to the underside of the arch itself. It is from this characteristic, repeated and insisted upon as it is all through the range of buildings of the period, that the style of building derives its name. This method divided the windows into similar rectangular shapes that lent themselves well to repetitive or mass-produced glazing, and each panel could be made to contain a separate picture of a story or a separate saint in a series, in stained glass. It is a satisfactory and dignified solu-

78

tion to the problem of window design on a vast scale.

The well-dressed stones that the masons were able to cut in this period gave the walls a clean, bare appearance that contrasts beautifully with the elaboration of the windows. Frequently in the more expensive buildings these wall surfaces were decorated both within and without with a delicate relief pattern, a repetition of the motifs that made up the tracery of the windows, making of the whole wall a pattern into which the windows fit as an integral part, rising to the culmination of perpendicular architecture, the roof.

Roofs in both stone and timber had by this time developed considerably. In late work, stone vaults were brought to a great pitch of refinement in which the fan-like springing of many ribs assumed the form of an inverted curved cone, like a trumpet standing on its mouthpiece. The ribs curved up and out to the semi-circular top of the cone that rested against those of the neighbouring cones, forming between them a series of almost flat diamond-shaped panels in the ceiling. The original diagonal ribs lost their importance and

many intermediate ribs, all of the same thickness, were introduced.

The vault ceased now to be a pointed tunnel intersected by other similar pointed tunnels and became a curved shell of great complexity. The calculations necessary to cut the stones for such a vault so that each fitted exactly into place are a measure of the skill of the 15th-century craftsmen.

The ribs of these vaults were formed into a panelled pattern that echoed the window tracery. All apparent structural quality in the roof had been lost in an ordered web of fine ribs. The structural principle is a direct

80

development of that of preceding vaulting, but based on the new arch forms, and with many more ribs than heretofore. This multiplicity of ribs then gave rise to the practice of cutting the panel and its rib from one piece of stone, the rib as such losing its former structural use and becoming a stiffener to the thin vaulting slabs rather than their support. Now that the rib was released from its first function it could be made to adopt shapes that were previously impossible.

For centuries the roofs of halls and smaller churches had been built in timber. It is in the Perpendicular period, however, that timber roofs become most highly developed. They are of all types, from the simple tie-beam roof to the elaborate double-tiered hammer-beam roof. It is the hammer-beam roof that takes pride of place. For splendour it has no equal. The great roof of

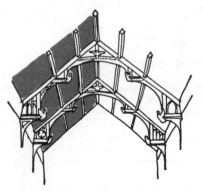

Hammer Beam Roof

Westminster Hall is the chief feature of the whole building, a fact that was evidently clearly realised by the designers, who kept the rest of the building extremely plain and simple in order to form the better contrast. The art of roof making was particularly highly developed in East Anglia, many Norfolk churches having splendid roofs quite out of proportion to their size and importance. The timbers of these roofs were usually brightly painted in many colours. This exposing, glorifying, and elaborating of the structural features of the roof is a very typical example of the medieval approach to building problems. The builder uses the structural necessities of his building as the basis of his design in the same way as he did with flying buttresses centuries ago.

In following the tendency towards simplicity, and a preference for rectangular shapes, the 15th-

century designer made the hood moulds over his doorways square, filling in the triangular space between the hood mould and the arch with simple cusping or other plain patterns, occasionally incorporating a coat-of-arms but never indulging in naturalistic foliage or realistic scenes. Flamboyance is wholly lacking in this type of design. It is all much more restrained, much less exuberant.

Pillars were frequently made up of several shafts that were merged together to such an extent as virtually to become mere mouldings on one shaft, mouldings that recall in their shallow curves and angles the

folds of pleated cloth. The capitals and bases tended towards straight-sided polygons, and the abolition of curves here is a noticeable feature.

Mouldings round arches tend to become rather thin, flat and mean, having none of the deep cut or voluptuous quality of the Early English or Decorated work. Carving, where it occurs, is of a highly formalised nature. A complete change has come about from the naturalism of the preceding century. Foliage is made to conform to a set geometrical design, and is frequently so changed and stylised as to be hardly recognisable as leaves, flowers, etc., at all.

Mock battlements are a very usual feature of this style of building. They are used over and over again, variously decorated, in almost all possible positions. The parapet-walls round roofs and towers are almost always embattled, but in a light-hearted way, the intention to decorate rather than to defend being perfectly obvious. The

liking for battlements went so far that they were frequently used in miniature as decorations to horizontal members of window tracery, carved screens, tombs, and so on, in either stone or wood as the occasion demanded. This form of decoration was popular possibly because it fitted so well with the prevalent custom of using rectangular panels as the basis for so much of the decoration. The parapets would frequently be carved with quatrefoils, lozenges, and circles, executed in bas-relief or inlaid with some contrasting material as split flint on stonework or dressed stone on brickwork, according to the local material with which the building was made. At Cirencester the parapet of the Guildhall is so carved as to become an open fretwork of stone, with tracery like the windows.

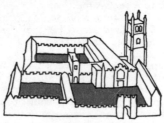

A University College

Perpendicular building is unlike any other building form, is very easily recognisable, and is wholly English. The 15th-century builders had a special genius for adding to existing buildings in the new style, harmonising with the old without accepting any of its form or detail. There are an immense number of churches that have been added to in the 15th century, besides many cathedrals. The new piece was invariably built on to the old as a direct contrast in proportion, style, and technique, and yet it nearly always looks well, and is an honest piece of work. Among many, a good example is

84

the large-scale alteration work at Winchester Cathedral, which is in startling contrast with the older work and yet lives side by side with it in perfect harmony.

The foundation of many university colleges was an indication of the trends of thought of the time. Learning was rapidly becoming less the exclusive property of the Church. The Renaissance movement was afoot.

PART TWO

Buildings of the Transitional Period

CHAPTER VI

RENAISSANCE (1501–1625)

THE RENAISSANCE was a rebirth of Greek and Roman ideas that supplanted medieval ways and thought. Its influence invaded every sphere of life, and caused a fundamental change in the appearance and planning of European buildings. The movement originated in Italy early in the 15th century, but its effects on the architecture of England did not become apparent until a century later. The Italian renaissance owed its inspiration to the works of the Romans, and Roman culture was based to a great extent on the civilisation of Ancient Greece. It is, therefore, in Greece that the story of Renaissance building really begins.

The large stones that could be cut from the Greek marble quarries had allowed the Ancient Greeks to use huge beams rather than arches. They preferred beams because they were more in keeping with their traditional timber construction, and were more satisfying aesthetically. Through centuries of trial and error the Greeks had evolved proportions for the various parts of their

CHISWICK HOUSE OR THE PALLADIAN VILLA

buildings designed exactly to satisfy their very highly developed aesthetic sensibilities. They made all their straight lines delicately curved to allow for optical illusions, and built their temples —their principal building type—to within an accuracy of a minute fraction of an inch. By the fifth century B.C. they had developed this beam-and-pillar building type to its final form, the most perfect example of their work being the Parthenon at Athens.

Greek Temple

The columns that the Greeks used were of three different sorts, varying with the different localities. Each sort of column had its own special proportions, mouldings, decorations, and so on, and the entire unit of construction and decoration is known as an Order. The three Orders are Doric, Ionic, and Corinthian.

Later the Romans conquered and colonised Greece. Being less concerned with aesthetic refinements but needing to build very much larger structures than could possibly be roofed over by the largest beam, the Romans adopted the arch as the structural basis of their buildings. However, they were so impressed by the superior culture and refinement of the Greeks, that they took their beam-and-pillar building motifs and in-

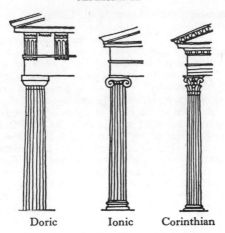

Doric   Ionic   Corinthian

corporated them into arch-and-dome constructed buildings as applied decoration, often quite oblivious of the function that they originally performed.

When the Romans adopted these motifs they abandoned the more delicate refinements and added some coarse and heavy-handed details of their own. Substantially, however,

Roman Arch

The Pantheon, Rome

the orders and general proportions remained the same. The ordinary details of Roman buildings were the semi-circular arch, the pediment, or Greek gable-end that they had adopted, and the three Orders now used

89

decoratively, often superimposed one on top of another in the various stages of a multi-storey building.

Early in the Christian era the Roman Empire collapsed, Rome herself was forsaken by the Emperor, who established his capital at Constantinople, and the greater part of Roman learning and philosophy was temporarily lost to the world. Greek culture, already dimming under Roman rule, suffered in the same collapse. Through the historical gloom of the Dark Ages that follow, wave after wave of heathen invaders sweeping across the stage in fierce and bloody battle may be but dimly seen. In this turmoil only the rock of Christianity stands firm, the rock on which was to be built the civilisation of Western Europe.

By the 13th century the great buildings of the ancient peoples were in ruins, skeletons of a forgotten past, used only as quarries for ready-made building material. But Italian writers of this date were already rediscovering the classical poets and philosophers, and were formulating a new conception of life on classical lines of reason and objective enquiry. The ever-present problem of reconciling medieval principles with man's growing knowledge of life as he saw and experienced it was gradually becoming more and more acute as his knowledge of ascertainable physical facts increased. As time went on men turned to the classics for a solution of this fundamental problem, and a full realisation of the heights of civilisation that had been reached by the ancients without the aid of any such medieval principles gave rise to grave doubts of their truth. By thought along these lines they prepared the ground for a revolt against the medieval outlook of mysticism and religious preoccupation.

Centuries later in far-off Constantinople an Easternised classical tradition was still strong. The old libraries of Constantine were still stocked with the works of the older civilisations. When in 1453 this city was sacked by the Turks, Western Europe, and particularly Italy, was flooded with refugees. Among them were many learned scholars who had escaped with a wealth of antique manuscripts and treasures from the libraries. It needed but this extra incentive to consolidate in a people already ripe for change an enthusiasm for classical culture. This was already becoming a ruling passion with influential Italians, who, by their patronage of the arts, enabled the splendid Italian architects, artists, and craftsmen of that time to execute many works in which they clearly expressed their enthusiasm for antiquity and the classical materialist outlook. Roman buildings were studied and surveyed, the ruins were reconstructed, grandiose Roman planning was admired and copied, and antique building forms became fashionable in the same way that classical

Italian Chapel

processes of thought were becoming universal. The new Italian buildings, however, were very different from the Roman buildings, for they fulfilled quite different purposes. But, being inspired by the enthusiasm for classical culture as interpreted by the 15th-century Italians, they always included some classical motifs such as the

Italian Villa

pediment, the dome, semi-circular arches, or straight beams, the Roman mouldings and the Roman columns.

On their journey from Italy to this country the new building forms suffered many changes. They came via France and the Netherlands, and were even further debased by the English builders,

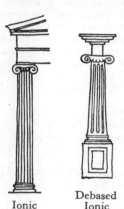

Ionic

Debased Ionic

who did not understand them, misapplied most of them, and were unaware of the exact proportions that the Greeks had worked out so long ago.

The initial stage of muddle and experiment that resulted did not last for more than a hundred years. Inigo Jones, who had studied the exact rules of classical proportions that had been formulated and tabulated by the Italian architect Andrea Palladio, was the first Englishman to build according to the correct rules. By the time of Jones' death in 1652, the period of transition from medieval to classic building was at an end.

The transition has been divided for convenience into two main parts, Tudor, which is largely medieval in detail but owes its *raison d'être* to the Renaissance movement, and Elizabethan and Jacobean, which is classic in detail, although at first very inaccurate in application and proportion. Although Elizabeth was a Tudor the architectural character of her reign falls more conveniently into the second category, and is indeed wholly different from the first.

During the medieval era we have learned to expect the structural problem to govern all and every part of the building. Now, in the 16th, 17th, and 18th centuries this basic consideration no longer so obviously applies, because the problems the builders had to solve were very much simpler. They seldom had to attempt such feats of engineering as the medieval church and cathedral builders, for not only were the majority of their buildings on the domestic scale, but they were not concerned to make them as light and dynamic as possible. To build in a "good Roman manner" was their aim, and the Romans relied on an appearance of great solidity to achieve their effects of magnificence. No longer were the lateral thrusts set up by arches and vaults of paramount importance except in the few really large buildings employing domes and arches. The lateral pressure of all but the largest arch could easily be absorbed in the more solid masonry that the new technique allowed.

Building forms no longer bore the close and obvious relationship to structural necessity that

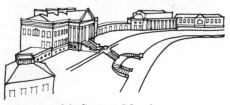

18th-Century Mansion

they did in medieval times, for they were forms arising from a long and involved history of change in which many had lost their original purpose, becoming applied decoration. Their admiration for the ancients gave the Renaissance builders the desire to adopt these features, and their rapidly increasing scientific knowledge gave them the structural ability to do so.

Here we enter on an age in which spiritual attainment is of secondary importance, intellectual ability paramount. It is a highly civilised age of great artificiality.

CHAPTER VII

TUDOR (1485–1560)

TUDOR BUILDINGS are wholly Gothic in form, but they are nearly all secular. This is scarcely surprising when the unpopularity into which the Church had fallen is considered, together with the fact that there were by this time plenty of churches for everyone. The dissolution of the monasteries provided large tracts of exploitable land on which farms were started by neighbouring gentry, who also built smaller farms and cottages for their tenants. At the same time Henry VIII was instituting a building programme—financed by the confiscated church properties and the prosperous wool trade—for large country mansions and palaces calculated to increase English prestige abroad.

Consequently, although the architectural character of this period is very much like the last, the accent is on domestic rather than ecclesiastical building, and so the scale is much more intimate. Windows and doors become smaller, buildings become more complicated, chimneys and fireplaces become common. The most characteristic feature of Tudor buildings, however, is the use of *brick*. This building material had suddenly acquired an almost universal popularity that spread from East Anglia. Some bricks were shipped across to this country from the Lowlands as ballast in the returning wool ships, and some were made in East Anglia by Belgian and Dutch brickmakers, who had set up yards there. Cardinal

Wolsey and Henry VIII both used brick for their palaces, and countless smaller houses and cottages were built of this new material.

Tudor Palace

The typical Tudor Great House presented a delightfully romantic appearance. Built in warm red brick, its most noticeable feature was the gate-house. This often consisted of a broad low arch flanked on either hand by tall octagonal towers, crowned with mock fortifications. Steep roofs and fantastic brick chimneys like cork-

screws, many gables and turrets, provided a variegated skyline. Above the door a coat-of-arms carved in brick or stone proclaimed the nobility of the owner, for many families at this time had only recently risen to wealth and power and thus ostentatiously displayed their new-found social status.

Castles were by this time quite unnecessary, and

any fortified buildings of this period were just so much stage scenery to provide what their owners considered a suitable background for their position and wealth.

The interiors of Tudor mansions are usually panelled from the floor almost to the ceiling with narrow panels each made of one plank of oak,

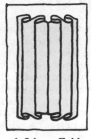

A Linen-Fold
Panel

which are either plain or are carved in the characteristic pattern known as linen-fold. The fireplace is a huge open affair with a four-centered arch over it, and in the houses of the wealthy there is usually a coat-of-arms or some other decorative feature carved in stone, wood, or brick as an overmantel. The chimney-stack was introduced at this period largely because of the new fuel—coal. This was found to produce an intolerable smoke. Wood smoke previously was allowed to get out of the house through the roof, or in the larger halls—in castles and the like—a large open fireplace with a rudimentary flue leading obliquely through an outside wall was usual.

97

Now, however, the necessity for taking the smoke right away above the house served a useful purpose, for the builders discovered that the fireplace need no longer occupy an outside wall, and that, with a flue taken up vertically from the hall, the great high room, open to the rafters, could now be floored in half-way up, so doubling the available floor space. The new floor was usually left bare underneath, showing between the beams on which it rested, without a plaster ceiling.

The windows are small, their size being governed by the domestic scale and the most convenient size for making an opening casement in iron and glass. They are simple and of a characteristic proportion, and are either single or grouped in pairs or threes with a stone or brick hood over them. They have flat arched heads, cut, more often than not, from one piece of stone, and the triangular spaces in the corners are nearly always cut out in little three-cornered depressions that may be regarded as the last faint remnants of tracery. These windows were normally built of stone let into the brickwork. Larger windows were of the perpendicular sort,

ST. JAMES'S PALACE: EARLY 16TH CENTURY

with tracery and stained glass as before. The oriel window was much used, and became somewhat larger and more elaborate.

Tudor arches are invariably either four-centered or a modification of the four-centered arch, which is flatter and has straight sloping members rather than curved ones.

As yet nothing has been said of timber buildings, and it would not be correct to leave the impression that all Tudor work is in brick. In timber districts such as Lancashire, Cheshire and Warwickshire, oak-framed houses were the rule, the details of windows and doors being carved in wood as though they were stone, that is, with little wooden arches and mouldings. A strong oak skeleton was set up and in between the timber members were built light panels of either brick or plaster, according to what local material was available. Often the brickwork in these panels was laid in decorative patterns, either in herring-bone or vertically. This could be done because the bricks were not used structurally but purely as an infilling to keep out the weather. In Tudor work the timbers were always placed very close together with little room for the infilling between. As yet the builders were uncertain of their material, not daring to build the more widely spaced and economical frames that were later adopted. Very often the lower storey was built in brick or stone, with the top storey and roof in timber. The combination of various materials is one of the most delightful features of the Tudor small house.

In districts where bricks were scarce or where plaster was easily made the famous black-and-white type of building resulted; black beams with whitewashed plaster panels in between. The upper floors of these houses frequently projected beyond the ground floors, giving them their characteristic overhang. This was particularly the case in towns where ground space was limited. Often houses were built of many stories, each storey projecting beyond the one below till houses on either side of the street practically touched. This practice was discontinued in Jacobean times.

Tudor House

In stone districts the local material was again used to the exclusion of brick, and such alterations in style as were necessitated by a different material are apparent. In country districts where there is a strong conservative building tradition details are seldom a true guide to date. Smaller buildings were still completely Gothic in character for years after the Renaissance, and the detailed history of a locality must be studied before allotting a building to a specific historical period. It is to this fact that the popular misconception with regard to the date of small houses is due. Comparatively few cottages are more than three hundred and fifty years old.

Before leaving the Tudor period mention must be made of one of the most remarkable buildings in England—Henry VII's chapel at Westminster. This was erected after his death and was executed in the most lavish manner possible. All the features are essentially perpendicular in form, but with none of the restraint noticeable in the earlier work. Here every part of the building is carved and decorated in a labyrinthine multitude of panels. The pinnacle has given place to a most characteristic Tudor motif, the stone, dome-shaped, pepperpot-like top to the buttresses. From the roof  stalactites of wrought stone seemingly hang—in reality the larger pendants actually support the vaulting—but the elaboration of carved work and the complication of the structural principles used so obscure the underlying meaning of the roof that the real magnificence of the engineering feat that the Tudor masons achieved is not apparent. The roof was designed in this elaborate manner in order to make the fashionable flat-headed window extend right up to the underside of the vault. The chapel is a marvellous work of craftsmanship and ingenuity and, although it does not necessarily represent the highest achievement of Gothic art, it is the Gothic building carried to its last stage. Development from here could clearly go no further. A dead end had been reached. By this time the Renaissance movement in Italy was already some hundred years old, and occasionally Italian craftsmen accepted commissions for works of art for wealthy or royal foreign patrons. In later years, during the time of the religious persecutions under Elizabeth and Mary, this practice was largely discontinued, or at best was only possible for artists upholding the faith of the reigning sovereign of the time. In this case, however, the Italian craftsman Pietro Torrigiano was commissioned to execute the tomb of Henry VII, which forms the centre-piece of the chapel and is the earliest well-known example of Renaissance work in the country.

The contrast between the simple humanity of the cherubs that sit at the corners of the tomb and the encrusted magnificence of the medieval structure that surrounds them is a remarkable example of the essentially different standpoints of the Gothic and Renaissance designers.

CHAPTER VIII

ELIZABETHAN AND JACOBEAN
(1560–1620)

AFTER THE death of Henry VIII less building was undertaken, for the king's spendthrift policy had left the country practically bankrupt. However, at the accession of Elizabeth the religious turmoil was largely quelled, and the prosperity of the country began to revive. The wool trade was not so prosperous as it had been, and the Queen wisely encouraged the farmers to increase their arable land as a change from sheep farming. This necessitated the employment of far more labour on the farms, and an increase in small houses and cottages resulted. The new policy succeeded well enough and the country again enjoyed a considerable measure of prosperity. Wealth was now distributed among a very much larger class of reasonably well-to-do people rather than concentrated into a few hands, a fact that further augmented the boom in small house building. Considerable big building in the form of new country mansions also took place, and many older houses were altered and modernised. Hospitality was considered of prime importance,

Elizabethan
Small House

THE TOMB OF THE POOLE FAMILY, SAPPERTON, GLOS.: EARLY 17TH CENTURY and the new aristocracy used to vie with one another, and half ruin themselves, in their attempts to make their homes the most fitting resting-

Elizabethan Cottages

places for the queen on her royal visits. The tremendous popularity of the sovereign was part of a great upsurge of patriotic feeling brought about by the successful defeat of the attempted Spanish invasion.

Great houses began now to be tricked out in all the fashionable details of what passed in Eliza-bethan England for Italian Renaissance. The Italian craftsmen attracted to the court of Henry VIII were giving place to Protestant Lowlanders, for the Catholics had thought it wiser to withdraw.

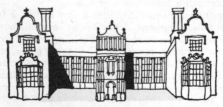

Elizabethan Mansion

The great trade that had been carried on with the Netherlands made this association a natural one, and printed illustrated books of architectural details from these countries were much used by English builders.

The development of the large houses continued from the manors of the Tudor period. The chief features of the Elizabethan great house were an effect of symmetry in the facade, a long gallery, an imposing staircase, and a formal garden incorporating such features as yew walks, terraces, and fountains. The symmetrical layout is the first indication of a change towards the classical plan.

The country had for some time been peaceful enough for the enclosed courtyard to be dispensed with, the gate-house, if built at all, being only for display. The layout had thus gradually assumed an E-shape, the vertical stroke representing the

The E Plan

main hall, the two long horizontals the sides of the old courtyard—now incorporated into the kitchens on the one hand and the old living-rooms on the other—and the short horizontal being the entrance porch, moved to the centre for the sake of symmetry. The "hall" became a large imposing entrance hall and was less and less used for living in, while the staircase that usually led from the hall was of the open-well rectangular sort, often with an elaborately carved balustrade and newel posts. The long gallery—obscure in origin and purpose—was placed on the first floor, and was a feature that the wealthy man of the time seemed reluctant to do without. The fundamental change that had come about here was that the hall and the living-rooms had changed places in their relative importance. The hall had become relatively unimportant, whereas such rooms as the long gallery had become the chief features of the house. Usually built in stone, for with the Renaissance movement brick was losing popularity for important buildings, with curved Dutch gables or else with a straight, balustraded parapet and a wealth of classical detail, the Elizabethan mansion

is nothing if not imposing. Chimneys were usually grouped in pairs or threes, were often made to resemble classic columns, and were usually rectangular instead of the fantastic corkscrew shapes of the preceding period. Windows are larger than ever before, consisting of a simple grid of vertical mullions and horizontal transomes with diamond-shaped or square leaded panes between. The windows have no arches but are completely rectangular, and are topped either with a Gothic dripstone or with a classical moulding.

It is by the mixture of Gothic ideas, like the hood mould over a window, with classical detail such as columns, broken pediments, and so forth, that Elizabethan work is most easily distinguished. It is always the necessary functional details of a building that cling longest in the older idiom, for whereas the craftsman is willing to try his hand at a new thing provided that should it prove unsatisfactory no disastrous consequences will follow, he is most reluctant to attempt to change from his traditional way of, for instance, keeping the rain out of a window. So in the embellishment of fireplaces and all internal fittings we see the earliest changes towards the new fashions, and in the deep-rooted basic structural idea of the house the Gothic tradition lingers longest.

The architectural expression of the Renaissance movement in England was as yet only in the form of fashionable decoration. No funda-mental change had been made in planning except for a tendency towards symmetry. It was not till Inigo Jones came home from Italy that the Italian style began to influence the basic shape of buildings.

The front doors to the houses of the wealthy expressed in their elaboration the prevailing spirit of hospitality and ostentation. This feature was made the most elaborate part of the house. Almost invariably it had a round semi-circular arch flanked by classic columns of dubious parentage and was often surmounted by a fantastic pile of carved stonework, incorporating the arms of the owner, statues of classical heroes, pinnacles, and all manner of carved work.

The smaller homes continued in the Tudor tradition and adopted the Renaissance decorative motifs much more slowly. Fireplaces and chimney-stacks now became common, and a larger staircase than the previous rude, ladder-like affair was incorporated. Otherwise the plan remained very much the same as it was before, with the central hall now floored in half-way up, flanked on either hand by the living-quarters and the kitchens. Timber buildings were more efficiently and economically constructed, the timbers now being spaced more widely apart.

In Jacobean times, when for reasons of safety from fire the king decreed that the overhanging houses that were such a characteristic feature of towns should no longer be built in London, the practice of building the frame in one single piece from ground to eaves became general.

The most characteristic detail of Elizabethan and Jacobean work is the use of strap ornament.

This, used lavishly both externally and internally on almost all features, is of Germanic origin, and usually takes the form of a bas-relief geometrical pattern of interlacing straps that is unmistakable.

Sometimes the motif was applied in fretwork to a balustrade, sometimes classical foliage is flavoured with a strap-like quality, and nearly always the pattern is sugared with a liberal sprinkling of lozenges, ovals, and diamonds, like jewels in a fancy-dress crown.

Columns often have a strange growth of decoration that climbs like ivy up a tree-trunk to as much as a third of their height. With regard to the details of the interiors, the walls of rooms were nearly always panelled in oak or decorated with panels of moulded plaster. These were often in patterns based on the round-arch form, or in later work were plain but for classical cornice mouldings round the top. Imported coloured marbles were much in vogue for decorative fireplaces, and black and white marble was imported to make chessboard floors to the halls of the wealthy. Ornament had run completely wild —fat classical columns and Gothic heraldry being inextricably mixed with cupids and strap ornament.

In Jacobean times the character of the work becomes a degree more classical but a great deal more Teutonic in flavour. The strap ornament gives way to a formalised foliage, and heavy-busted female caryatids are all too frequently employed on columns that are larger at the top than at the bottom.

Decorative plaster ceilings were much in fashion in the Elizabethan mansion. Most of the patterns were derived from late Gothic fan vaulting, and pendants in miniature imitation of those in the roof of Henry VII's chapel at Westminster were used as a decoration, hanging like stumpy stalactites from the intersections of the plaster ribs.

As the 17th century progressed, so the quality of the decorative work became more correct. By the time Inigo Jones died much of the more gross and vulgar features of Stuart detailing had given place to a sober but ponderous classicism.

PART THREE

Buildings of the Classical Era (1620–1800)

CHAPTER IX

INIGO JONES AND CHRISTOPHER WREN (1620–1720)

DURING THE first three-quarters of the 17th century only a few large buildings were undertaken because of the social and religious upheavals that were taking place. It is during this period, however, that individual architects became of importance. Buildings were planned, not by members of organisations such as the Church in which their names became lost, but by independent architects or architects holding a post under the Crown. Architecture now became dependent more on mind and intellect than on craftsmanship and material.

At the beginning of the century there was little accurate knowledge of classical proportions or usage. No one had made a sufficiently careful study of ancient buildings, or of the laws that Palladio had evolved from them, to build anything that was not a very debased and second-hand

---

version of classic proportion. Inigo Jones was the first man to bring the pure Italian Renaissance style to this country. He was an architect who had studied in Italy for some years, and was appointed as Surveyor-General of the Works in 1615, making him chief architect to the Crown. The style he built in was pure Italian with as few modifications as possible. His buildings were very un-English in character, with the severe flat line of the parapet which hid the roof, and the solemn, regularly spaced columns along the front. His two most revolutionary designs were the Banqueting Hall in Whitehall and the Queen's House at Greenwich. The latter was of great

Queen's House, Greenwich

importance, for nothing had been seen like it in England before, not only in its strict classical details but in its general shape. The plan and conception of this house profoundly influenced all subsequent domestic design. It was completely rectangular, having no gables or other projections, it was completely symmetrical, and it had the principal rooms on the first floor. This last was an Italian fashion, lending added height and magnificence to the building by giving it a tremendously solid-looking ground floor on which the main floors could rest, as on a massive base. The rooms on the first floor were very high and grand, with large windows, and the layout gives great scope for magnificence in the staircase. This device of raising the whole house up one floor became so popular a method of giving a sense of importance to buildings that it lasted right up to the end of the 19th century, by which time the original conception deteriorated into the familiar half-basement, but still retained a remnant of the grand manner in the short flight of steps up to the front door. Inigo Jones designed in accordance with Palladio's rules of classic proportion only under considerable difficulties, for he had to persuade his builders and masons to forsake all their traditional ideas of how to go about their work in favour of his own. Up till this time masons had had a comparatively free hand in the details they carried out. The main lines of the design were indicated to them and they were allowed, within those lines, very considerable scope. This resulted in individual and interesting detailed work in a building, but the details were seldom, if ever, "correct" or according to any given set of rules. Now, however, Inigo Jones was working within a rigidly laid down convention, and he had to insist on his masons interpreting his drawings accurately, a most difficult and unusual task.

Inigo Jones had little influence on architectural design during his lifetime, and houses continued to be built in the Jacobean manner up to the time of his death. Nevertheless, his influence was to be profound, for men like Christopher Wren and all those who followed him owed their basic conception of classic design to the pioneer work done by Inigo Jones.

The problem that now arose was how to adapt

this new foreign building technique to English ways and English climate, English materials and English craftsmen. To Inigo Jones this problem was of secondary importance. Several country houses were designed and altered by him, or at least owe their form to his immediate influence.

A House after Inigo Jones

Here the steep roofs and the vast chimneys sit somewhat awkwardly over the classic façade. As yet the Italian and the native idioms are at variance. Such English features as steeply pitched roofs, chimney-stacks, large windows, and all the parts of a building that owe their character to a cold, dull, damp climate had to be fitted to the new style. Could this problem be resolved whilst still retaining the richness, dignity, and repose that are the results of true classical proportion? Christopher Wren was the man who, to a great extent, achieved the solution.

This immensely versatile man was a mathematician, an astronomer, and, above all, an inventor. It is to his enquiring inventiveness that so much of his success is due. He used traditional English building materials, brick and ordinary roofing-tiles, inventing new ways of using these in order to keep within the limits of classic rules. He also popularised the use of Portland stone in London.

Brick and Stone Combined

He, like Inigo Jones, was appointed Surveyor-General to the Crown when he was about thirty years old, and started almost immediately on the immense task of rebuilding the churches of London, burnt down in the Great Fire of 1666. The immediate rebuilding of these churches shows that if little church-building had been done in the 17th century, it was because there were already enough churches for everyone rather than that people were indifferent to religious matters. It should be stressed, however, that the house remains the predominant building type of the 17th and 18th centuries, and that next in importance after the house comes a great quantity of public and commercial building, such as customs-houses,

A Customs House

121

hospitals, pump-rooms, market-places, shops, and so on. The church building of London was mostly accidental because of the Fire, although, of course, some churches were built to meet the needs of the growing suburbs.

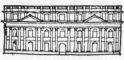

A Hospital

By the end of the 17th century, services in the reformed Protestant Church were very different affairs from the old medieval ones. Gone was the sense of mystery, gone the barrier between the priest and the congregation. The new conception of a church was a large room in which as many people as possible could hear the preacher in comfort, a room that was full of light and clarity and common sense. Wren's interiors are clean, beautiful rooms, with gold-and-white plaster work and large pale windows; with galleries round the walls for the extra people that lived in a crowded city. The altar, a simple puritan table, was often in the body of the church rather than at

A Market Place

the east end. It is a building fit for a service in which the importance of the spoken word—the sermon—is paramount, rather than one in which may be held the mystic ritual of the older faith.

Wren's planning of these churches, his squeezing of them into almost impossibly small places and obtaining in spite of this such a feeling of spaciousness and rest, is among his greatest achievements. Outside, these buildings are nearly always very simple, and are usually crowned by spires or towers that rise above the roof tops of London and mark the parishes. It is by these spires that Wren's churches are chiefly known. They are tall piles of beautifully proportioned stone and are very ingenious, for classical motifs are here welded into what is after all essentially a Gothic shape, and they show in their structure the greatest engineering cunning.

The Queen Anne House

A City Spire

The construction of the dome of St. Paul's Cathedral is an engineering feat comparable with the greatest that the Italian architects had achieved.

But apart from his churches, as has already been said, Wren influenced the design of houses, both in town and country, and it was under his influence that, at the beginning of the 18th century, the characteristic Queen Anne house evolved.

To fit the classical way of building to the ordinary well-to-do gentle-

Queen Anne Town House

man's home, that is, to build a house that was not a palace but still retained all the simple dignity of a classical design, was the problem solved for the first time in the Queen Anne house.

In this type of design gables were undesirable, and hipped roofs were used instead, a roof that sloped up from the eaves to the ridge from all four sides, thus preserving the horizontal eaves line all round the building. The eaves line was treated like a cornice, with the small curly brackets in imitation of the carved ends of rafters that are found on ancient Roman buildings. If the number of floors that a certain house needed meant that the house would look too high for its width, that is, too high a shape to conform with the laws of proportion that the design demanded, the top floor was put above the eaves in the roof, the windows projecting through in the form of dormers, leaving the heavy horizontal line of the eaves or cornice uninterrupted at the lower level. The dormers were often given little pediments, either curved or triangular. Sometimes they had a

miniature steep-pitched roof of their own. These devices were used by Inigo Jones and his pupil, Webb, but without Wren's delicacy and homeliness of proportion.

These houses, following the Queen's House at Greenwich, were nearly always of a simple rectangular shape, and were to all outward appearances completely symmetrical. Only in the more pretentious houses were the principal rooms put on the first floor. Built in the local materials, either stone or brick, they fitted well into the English countryside. Their angles were frequently treated with quoins, or corner stones, or with blocks of brickwork, alternately long and short, projecting slightly from the surface of the wall.

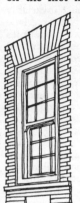

Their windows had heavy wood or stone frames, thick glazing bars, and the same long and short pattern on a smaller scale worked up the sides in a slightly raised or darker brick. At their head, a stone or raised brick keystone was often introduced, and their flat arches were occasionally decorated with a "cupid's bow" type of scroll.

The feature which has influenced our urban landscapes more than any other is undoubtedly the sash window, introduced early in the 18th century. It is to be seen in many Queen Anne houses, became almost universal in the Georgian period, and remained the standard domestic window until the end of the 19th century. This ingenious mechanism

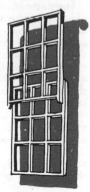

shows clearly the new scientific approach of the contemporary designers.

Queen Anne doorways were almost invariably given canopies, supported on characteristic brackets. These canopies were sometimes straight and sometimes curved in the form of pediments. All manner of light-hearted variations were adopted, a frequent and delightful device being to make them so deep and round that their insides could be treated like shells. These doorways were usually made of wood or stone, but in town houses the whole elaborate design was sometimes built up in fine brickwork. In this case the pediment was usually supported on half columns instead of brackets.

Inside the houses of the wealthy, the ceilings, if decorated, had heavy plaster garlands of fruit, flowers, and vegetables running round them in ponderous geometrical patterns. Carving of this sort was "in the round," almost standing free from its background, and all the fruit, dead partridges, potatoes, and so on that were incorporated were treated with the utmost realism. Chimney-pieces were in the same character as the doors, being heavily framed in marble with deep curly mouldings, and possibly a pediment on top. In later work they were simpler, and relied on wood rather than stone for their effect. The character of the rooms was dignified and solid, the walls panelled in large deep panels, the ceiling in heavy solemn patterns.

The 17th century was one in which architectural character made considerable changes, but in different degrees at different levels. The poor man's house had hardly changed at all, but was slowly becoming less medieval in its details and was built of more permanent materials. It remained, however, essentially the same as it had been in the past. On the other hand, the rich man's house had changed completely from the higgledy-piggledy layout of the last century, with battlements and turrets, oriel windows, and clipped yew hedges, to the symmetrical, steep hip-roofed mansion, ponderously chimneyed, with its square windows framed like pictures and its solemn tall rooms. Again, churches had conformed to the requirements of a new form of religion, and were clothed in all the frills of the new building technique, a change that is perhaps more startling than that of the house, since the evolution was more spasmodic.

In the next century we shall see the further development and refinement of these tendencies, the growth of the town house and of town planning, and the beginning of the industrial revolution.

THE CROSS BATHS AND BATH STREET, BATH : LATE
18TH CENTURY

CHAPTER X

THE EIGHTEENTH CENTURY
(1720–1800)

EIGHTEENTH CENTURY building is characterised by its great refinement. It is the architecture of a highly civilised age. The predominating building type that flavours the whole century is the Town House. This, the Georgian terrace house, was built in very great numbers and was to a high

18th-Century Houses

degree standardised, because during this century there existed an accepted standard of good taste. The general acceptance of one standard was possible because one philosophy was believed, a philosophy of materialism and of reason. It was a somewhat circumscribed and brittle philosophy in which there was little room for half-tones. A thing was either right or wrong. This applied to all activities, and in the sphere of architecture it implied that there was only one right way to build. This was the standard; to depart from it would be bad taste—almost bad manners. The house, although the principal type, was far from being the only sort of building.

The 18th century is one packed with incident, and great numbers of all classes of buildings, including shops, public works, and commercial buildings, were erected.

A Public Building

The wealth of the country was once more concentrated into fewer hands. The rich were becoming prodigiously wealthy, and owned huge tracts of land, often as much as half a county, which they enclosed rigidly. Common land became scarce, and consequently the livelihood of the smallholder became more precarious. The only way of life left to him was either to work as a labourer for the big landowner or to seek employment elsewhere. The towns, which were centres of growing commerce, absorbed many of these smallholders and a depopulation of the countryside gradually began.

Within his enclosed land the wealthy man laid aside enormous areas as private parks in which to keep ornamental deer and trees and in which to build his house. So powerful were these men that they were able to remove a whole village and build it elsewhere, if it were in the way of their grandiose schemes. They laid out their parks with wonderful avenues of huge trees many miles long and often hundreds of yards broad, down which could be seen vistas of rolling grass, cunningly punctuated with artificial lakes and delicate sophisticated classical monuments—little temples, bridges, wells, or grottoes—and so contrived as to terminate in some outstanding local

The Avenue

feature, such as a church tower or a hill. If no such feature existed, one would be built—a triumphal arch, an imitation ruin, a mausoleum, or an obelisk. For such men no flight of fancy was too extravagant, but it was extravagance on the grand scale: no tawdry spend-thrift whim of the moment, but an extravagance on a long-term policy. None of the great landscape artists of this time can ever have seen his schemes as he meant them to be seen, for none of the splendid

A Mausoleum

avenues would have reached anything approaching maturity when he died. Life in the 18th century must have seemed wonderfully secure for such plans to have been conceived and carried out, for a private fortune spent willingly on posterity argues a remarkable faith in the future.

In the early part of the century these great houses were often designed in the Baroque manner, employing classical motifs freely to produce an effect of grandeur, without regard for the strict rules of proportion.

The Baroque, as a term applied especially to an architectural type rather than to a form of decoration as is its more general sense, implies a style that owes little to convention and all to effect. It appeals, almost brutally, to the senses and hardly at all to the intellect. The designer allows his imagination to run riot, and produces splendid

compositions in stone and brick of a dreamlike, often nightmarish, quality. Its critics call it theatrical, referring to its almost scenic quality, but the art of the theatre is essentially two-dimensional, creating occasionally the illusion of three dimensions, the charm of which lies in the fact that the beholder is well aware of the illusion. The Baroque is immensely three-dimensional, producing in the onlooker a strong consciousness of the mass of the building and of the space enclosed within it.

Sir John Vanbrugh and Nicholas Hawksmoor were the chief exponents of Baroque in England, where it was never very popular. The British taste for understatement and lack of ostentation is probably responsible for this unpopularity, for Baroque owes a great part of its attraction to a magnificent

exaggeration. Although great size is by no means an essential quality of this style of building, in Vanbrugh's hands it became titanic. In his palaces, Cyclopean columns overshadow great mountains of masonry, so solid as to take the breath away. Blenheim Palace and Castle

Blenheim Palace

Howard are his two greatest works. They rely for their effect of magnificence not on a profusion of rich and fussy details, but on their broad massing and heroic proportions. Few mortals could hope to live up to such Olympian homes.

The 17th and 18th century gentleman delighted to immortalise himself in lavish tombs and many may be seen in the contemporary classic Baroque manner, contrasting strangely with the sober Gothic churches in which they are situated.

Nicholas Hawksmoor's chief works were churches. He continued where Wren had left off, building such churches as were necessary for the rapidly growing suburbs of London. He built in the free inventive style of Wren, but without his warmth and genius.

After Wren, Vanbrugh, and Hawksmoor had

died, the spirit of experiment and invention died too. Architecture settled down to a conventional good taste, a return to a taste which conformed more strictly to the Palladian principles introduced by Inigo Jones. Palladian features such as doors, windows and mouldings may be seen in buildings of almost any date from the middle of the 17th century onwards.

A Palladian Doorway

Large houses, although they continued to be laid out with considerable extravagance, became in themselves less generous, more cold and aloof; they have an air of aristocratic superiority quite at variance with the bombast of the Baroque.

18th-Century Mansion

Meanwhile, what of the less fabulously wealthy? As has already been pointed out, these we can expect to find in the towns.

Prosperous towns as trading centres, like

Norwich and Bristol, or as fashionable resorts, such as Bath, were growing rapidly. London itself was expanding at a great pace. Towards the end of the 17th century the density of houses in towns had given rise to the invention of the terrace as a means of preserving dignity suitable to the wealth of the occupant together with economy in space. By building a whole street of houses all run together and treated as an

A Georgian Terrace

architectural whole, comparatively small houses could be given all the dignity of a palace. Thus we see in London, first in the Temple and other Inns of Court, built before the end of the 17th century, later in proper houses, the first terraces; the first of what was to become in the 18th century the general method employed for a vast residential urban development.

Eighteenth-century terraces took the form of simple brick buildings with stone tops to their parapets which hid the sloping slate roofs. In London and clay districts they were invariably of brick, but in stone districts, such as Bath, the local material was used. Between the houses were thick walls designed to prevent fire in one house spreading to the next, and which carried the chimney-stacks. These were made as unobtrusive as possible. Usually the houses were four stories high, with a short flight of steps up to the front door. Below the ground floor there was a basement, the principal rooms being on the first floor.

The standard details of such houses are a familiar sight in almost any town. The sash window was introduced early in the century and this was almost the only window employed in all but the remote country districts until the middle of the 19th century. Tall and dignified, with delicate wooden glazing bars glazed in standard-sized panes of glass, the Georgian window does much to harmonise whole districts of our towns. The proportion of these windows was beautifully calculated to produce a feeling of rest and dignity. Short windows on the ground floor for solidity, very tall windows on the first floor for grandeur, slightly shorter on the next, and at the top of the house completely square windows serve as a full stop to arrest the eye. In such subtleties of design the Georgian architects delighted and excelled. The front doors are generous and are

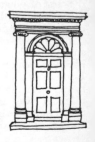

136

delicately panelled, with semi-circular fanlights over them. The sides of the brick opening in which they are set and the underside of the arch are often thinly plastered and painted cream, as are the sides of the window openings. Inside the front door a rectangular or oval stone staircase leads up, balustraded in fine wrought-iron.

The 18th-century builders laid out their terraces in simple straight streets, fine big squares, with gardens in the middle, in crescents and circuses, one opening out of the next, forming vistas and avenues of masonry and brickwork terminating in clumps of trees that are the square gardens, just as in the country they laid out avenues of trees, terminating in buildings. The insistence on vistas and avenues, which is a natural outcome of a symmetrical layout, was a technique that the Renaissance architects had taken from ancient Rome, and was a complete innovation to England. This fine planning was not for the nobility or the very wealthy; it was for a large and growing upper middle-class. Palaces in other countries may be finer than ours, churches may be larger, town halls may be grander, but in no other country in the world has such a

An 18th-Century Crescent

137

large section of its community been housed in such dignity.

Town-planning of this sort would not have been possible if every man had built his own house. The way it was done was that the original owner of the land—and huge tracts were in the possession of single land-owners—if he thought it profitable, would "develop" it as a speculation, laying it out as attractively as possible to captivate the wealthy tenants who would pay him a suitable rent. Sometimes these men would employ a contractor to carry out their own schemes; sometimes the contractor or architect would plan the whole layout as a private speculation of his own. Four architects, the two Woods and the two Dances, both fathers and sons, were responsible for developing large areas of Bath and Dublin respectively, while later in the century the brothers Adam did much to develop still more of Georgian London, and developed a style quite their own. By this time the design of terrace houses was to so standard a plan that it is only in the general layout and the details that one style changes from the next. Most of the Adams' work was

in town housing, and some of the terraces they laid out are among the most delightful in the country. They refined all the features of the Georgian town house, taking as the inspiration for their designs the details of Ancient Greece.

Adam doorways had beautiful spider's-web fanlights over them, the glazing bars made in cast lead ; windows were taller and with thinner glazing bars than ever before. Balconies were made of wrought-iron so fine that it was like fili-gree. Everywhere the Greek honeysuckle pattern was used, in plasterwork on the columns, which were now often made quite attached to the main build-ing and of a flat rectangular section, in the iron work of the

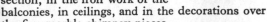

balconies, in ceilings, and in the decorations over the fine marble chimney-pieces.

A further aspect of the Georgian street

scene that is still a feature of many provincial towns is the large number of beautiful shop fronts. Arched, bowed, barrel-shaped, or plain, often still with their elegant lettering in gold on black, they lend us a tantalising glimpse of a more spacious and more leisured age.

Georgian Shop
Window

PART FOUR

Buildings of the Industrial Era
(1801 *to present day*)

CHAPTER XI

THE NINETEENTH CENTURY

THE ARCHITECTURE of the 19th century falls into three categories: Regency architecture, revival architecture, and what, for want of a better term, we shall call industrial architecture. The first belongs to the first thirty years of the century and is a direct continuation of the Georgian tradition of domestic building The second overlaps the first in time and is a

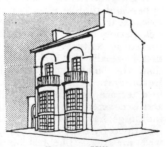

Regency Villa

phenomenon peculiar to the 19th and early 20th centuries, a powerful movement for reviving past

THE BRIDGE AT IRONBRIDGE, SALOP, 1779
THE FIRST LARGE IRON BRIDGE TO BE BUILT

styles, of erecting buildings for all purposes in the manner of past ages. The third runs as an undertone to the other two throughout the 19th century, and continues in the 20th, and is the outcome of experiment with new building materials. In this category fall such buildings as the Crystal Palace, the iron and glass railway stations, and the bridges of Telford, Brunel, and others.

Gothic Revival Church

During the Regency and the reign of George IV, upper and middle-class homes continued in the classical tradition. The domestic architecture of this period seems to belong in character to the preceding century. It is so refined and civilised that it recalls the Golden Age of culture rather than the smoke and turmoil of the Industrial Revolution. The typical Regency house, whether in a terrace or a detached villa, is built of brick and is covered in stucco or painted plaster. The buildings have a delicate Graeco-Italian flavour lent them by their refined proportion and painted wall surfaces. The fashion for stucco was imported from Italy and was originally intended to imitate stone, but in England it was used simply for what it was, a cheap, paintable, mouldable facing material. All the richness and refinement of Greek carving, fluted columns, complicated cornices, and the delicate folds of classical drapery, could be reproduced in shining, newly painted stucco at a fraction of the cost of worked stone. Even the small professional man could afford these elegant trimmings, and elegance is the essence of Regency architecture. Under the influence of Lord Elgin, Byron, and various amateur archaeologists, an enthusiasm had grown up for ancient Greek culture, a tendency that had already been foreshadowed in the Greek motifs employed by the Adam brothers. This revival of Greek taste invaded every sphere: dresses, interior decorative painting, furniture and building, all came under the spell. In the classical motifs employed on buildings the more heavy-handed Roman versions were replaced by the Greek. But the similarity with Greece ended there. Terraces were still laid out in the grand Roman manner, as those round Regent's Park by Nash. Many of these terraces are served by private carriage-ways entered through triumphal arches in stucco, are balanced by a symmetrical arrangement of pediments and side pavilions, and are fronted

A Nash Terrace

by rows of gigantic plaster columns. They are conceived on the grandest and most lavish scale.

The smaller and less pretentious terraces of the Regency, often also in stucco, are a less robust version of the Georgian terrace. They may be seen in great numbers in Cheltenham, Brighton, and London, besides many other towns less obviously influenced by the world of fashion of their

day. They have about them a faint air of decadence and insubstantiality. They have tall, thin windows with minutely small glazing bars, and in the grander and earlier examples, fine ironwork balconies made as delicate as gossamer, roofed in curving metal like a chinese pagoda. Decorative motifs are few, the terraces relying for their effect on their good proportions and pleasing painted walls. Round-headed ground-floor windows and front doors are usual in the later

and simpler terraces. The detached houses and small villas of the time are similar to the terraces, with fine ironwork verandas and garden windows that come down to the ground. Curved bow windows now came greatly into fashion and such towns as Portsmouth have any number of delightful local variations. Extravagantly low-pitched slate roofs and wide projecting eaves recall the warm Mediterranean, an effect that is further deliberately heightened by the use of painted wooden shutters.

For some time past a dilettante romantic movement had been afoot that found beauty in rusticity, a whimsical return to medievalism, and other exotic building forms. This had at first shown itself in such buildings as Gothic ruins in the grounds of the great landowners, carefully designed *cottages ornées* for their tenants, and such fashionable curiosities incorporated in their classical mansions as a Gothic library or dining-room.

Later this tendency takes a more serious, less light-hearted turn, and with its light-heartedness it loses its charm, and we are left only with the inconvenience.

The social evils that now resulted from the fearsome increase of industry and population were becoming all too evident. Grace, peacefulness, and dignity seemed no longer to exist in a world of ugliness, meanness, and squalor. Men of sensibility felt this state of affairs keenly, but instead of fighting the evil they attempted to escape it; instead of blaming their inability to control and organise the new world that was being created with the help of the machine, they blamed the machines themselves. They attempted to put the clock back, to return to what they thought of as the more genuine ways of the medieval era. They encouraged the making of articles by hand, tried to revive the medieval craft-guilds, and regarded all things made by machines as worthless. They tried to create for themselves a dream world divorced as far as possible from the unpleasant realities they despised. This was a counsel of despair and the dream turned out a nightmare. The characteristic that the pioneers of this movement admired in the Gothic was its structural honesty. Unfortunately, they did not apply that admirable quality to contemporary structures— using as the medieval builders would surely have done the new materials that were then available— so much as imitate the more sombre and morbid details of the Early English style. In this idiom was much Gothic revival building cast. Although the inception of the revival was due to such academic aesthetic principles, formulated by serious architects of great ability, its universal popularity was largely due to the romantic escapist tendencies that have already been mentioned. The impracticability and inconvenience of this style of building may be judged when we consider the Law Courts in London, the 19th-century school, or the local police station. Indeed, so

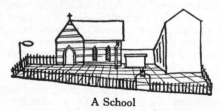

A School

inconvenient a medium was it found to be that the Houses of Parliament, though nominally dressed in the clothes of the Perpendicular Gothic, were given as their basic plan the long horizontal shape of a classical design.

The wealthy man's house was given a romantic

Gothic appearance, and since he could afford to have the thing done really well, it was no doubt quite successful. But what is fashionable in the wealthy of one generation is aped by the poor in the next. So the mock-medieval house descends every well-defined rung of the Victorian social ladder as the century progresses, and as the size of the house diminishes and the standard of craftsmanship that the builder can afford drops off, so the fashion becomes more and more ridiculous till we are confronted by the gimcrack bijou residence of the 1890's.

Cottage Residence

Meanwhile, it is not to be supposed that the medievalists held the field undisputed. The classicists and admirers of the Graeco-Roman tradition were not to be defeated without a fight. They continued building in the Renaissance manner, and tremendous arguments between what amounted to two separate camps took place, the classical against the medieval. In the end some sort of a compromise appears to have been reached, as during the last fifty years of the 19th and the first twenty of the 20th centuries, buildings of an ecclesiastical or scholastic character were

147

almost invariably Gothic, while business premises and civic buildings were usually in some sort of a ponderous classic style. The honours appear to have been divided fairly evenly over domestic buildings, while in the sphere of industry a sort of Romanesque with a tendency towards the Venetian in warehouses became the rule.

Greek Revival

The classicists returned to a fine Greek style of building which in itself became a revival, and many municipal buildings and even churches were erected almost as replicas, to outward appearances, of the buildings on the Acropolis of Athens. The Entrance to Euston Station is the modified façade of an enlarged Greek temple used with great effect as a triumphal arch, a conception entirely Roman.

Building in fancy-dress styles continued throughout the 19th century, the periods from which the styles were borrowed varying from time to time, Tudor, Jacobean, Perpendicular Gothic, Norman, Elizabethan, each having their share besides a host of other styles borrowed from abroad.

As time passes and we

Commercial Classic

148

can get these comparatively recent events into better focus it becomes more and more evident that there existed during the whole century other and what we believe will be more far-reaching influences. From the beginning of the century architects had concerned themselves less and less with practicalities and more and more with abstract artistic theory, with what results we have seen. Engineers now came into prominence as apart from architects. This was a distinction brought about by the supposed incompatability of industrial necessity and aesthetics, the engineers having to build bridges and railway stations and the architects refusing to have anything to do with subjects so low.

The engineers welcomed such new material as science made available. Sheet glass and cast iron (later steel) were the two most important new materials that had arrived in quantity by the middle of the century. These were used by Sir Joseph Paxton, who designed the Crystal Palace, a prefabricated building made entirely of standard sheets of glass and standard girders of iron. The railway companies were not slow to see the possibilities of such a structure applied to a railway terminus, a building inside which whole trains could steam and that could have a roof so immensely high up that the smoke from the engines would hardly affect it. They enclosed in these shells of iron and glass enormous volumes of space, giving rise to an entirely new sensation in the beholder, creating buildings large enough for atmospheric effects to come into play. Railway bridges of an immense size were constructed of iron and steel. The Forth Bridge, completed in

1890, takes its place as one of the really great bridges in the world. It is over a mile-and-a-half long and in a single span reaches one-third of a mile.

The Forth Bridge

Great architecture is never divorced from engineering, but few engineers are trained to aesthetic refinements of proportion, texture and colour, form composition and material, of which the architect is at all times acutely aware. There is always a choice of materials and forms that is open to the designer of any structure, and it is the successful choice of these in many of the engineering works of the 19th century which raises them from the sphere of good and efficient engineering to that of great architecture.

Towards the end of the century commerce and urban populations had greatly increased, so that larger building became necessary. Huge offices were needed, large blocks of flats, big shops, and banking houses. In crowded cities it was necessary to build high, and this led to the invention of the steel frame; the first steel-frame building in London being built in 1906.

Just as the most economical way of building a timber house in medieval times had been to set up a wooden skeleton and fill in between the bones with a light wall to keep out the weather, so now the same system was adopted on a huge scale with steel. But popular taste, with a leaning towards the pompous and traditional, insisted that such skeletons be clothed in massive stonework so that to all outward appearances the building should represent a classical façade of great solidity and worth. Such shams—for they are no less—are so common a feature of our towns today that we are no longer shocked at the spectacle of piles of solid masonry supported, apparently, by nothing more substantial than a plate-glass window.

Nothing has been said of the poor man's house, the cottage of the 19th century. The population had increased so rapidly that even at the beginning of the century thousands of new working-class homes were needed in the industrial areas. The increase continued throughout the century and more and more houses were built. On the first half of the century falls the blame for creating the slums of industrial England. It was an unprecedented problem that arose almost before anyone realised it existed, and the flood, once

Miners' Cottages

fairly started, could not be stemmed. The endless rows of exactly similar ill-built, depressing insanitary houses to which so much publicity has rightly been given during the last fifty years, constituted an environment as horrible as any that man has ever devised.

The 19th century was one of great contrasts. Pomp and splendour and appalling squalor on the one hand; and on the other a welter of insincerity, imitation, and fancy-dress building contrasted sharply with splendid feats of engineering.

Gothic Revival

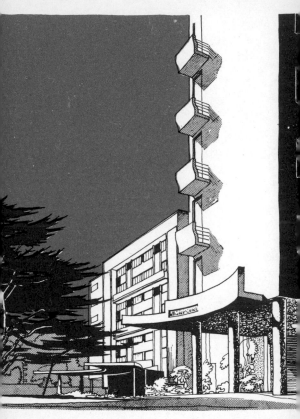

FLATS AT HIGHGATE: 20TH CENTURY

CHAPTER XII

THE TWENTIETH CENTURY

THE BEGINNING of the 19th century saw the emergence of the engineer designer in contrast to the architect designer. Canals, canal bridges and tunnels, improved roads and road bridges and later railways, demanded a different approach to design from that of the architect as he then was. Designers who thought in terms of technology became the engineers; those who thought in terms of academic aesthetic formulae became the architects, and no love was lost between what soon became the two opposed modes of thought.

Towards the end of the 19th century a few architects, realising how absurd this state of affairs was and how far from fulfilling contemporary needs they were with their revivalist designs, determined to make a fresh start and evolve more genuine solutions to building problems in full collaboration with engineers. In order to break away from the applied period styles that had by the end of the century become the accepted meaning of architecture, these men reverted to first principles and a dogmatic adherence to the functionalist ideal, believing that if a thing was truly fitted to its purpose it must necessarily be beautiful. This belief was an improvement on that of the revivalists, who appeared to hold that in order to be beautiful a building must be built in the manner of a past age. Functionalism alone, however, could not produce great architecture for it overlooked other factors of importance such as

155

form, proportion and texture; but it did achieve its purpose. It revitalised architecture and produced what we have called, for want of a better term, the modern tradition.

The fundamental principles of design underlying architecture today are, as they have been in other great ages, *truth* and *economy of means*. If a building looks what it is, and appears to be made as it is made, and to do what it does do; if no more material has been used than is required for its special function; then, however unsuccessful that design may be, it can be criticised and classified as within the modern tradition. If these conditions cannot be said to have been

A Contemporary
Factory

fulfilled, then no matter how pleasing the result, the building fails to be modern in the true sense of the word. We must never forget that *all* buildings in this land, whether factories, churches, houses or even blast furnaces and silos, are "architecture" in the sense that they are designed structures. Few will care in future years whether the builders of these structures were termed architects, engineers or otherwise. They will be there for all to see as the "architecture" of the 20th century. Principles therefore are important.

An example will help to illustrate what we mean by "truth" in relation to architecture. Stone has been used from time immemorial for the building of walls; dressed stones bonded together are what for centuries we have become used to and associate with strength, because to bond the stones together is the true way of making the wall strong. Now that steel and concrete skeletons are the basic structure of large buildings, walls need no longer be strong—they carry no weight. To clothe the structure in bonded stone-work must be a waste of material and a sham. Through force of habit our eye has come to expect bonded stonework—and during the first half of the 20th century architects clothed their frameworks in bonded stone, giving the walling a spurious air of solidity. Osbert Lancaster has described the framed building and the solid structure building as vertebrate and crustacean; the two should never be confused. Stone may, however, be sawn or split very thin and the slabs cramped on to the framework as a facing. This is only appropriate if the stones are jointed and arranged to look not like solid masonry but the applied facings that they are. This is of course only one very small instance to illustrate the application of the abstract quality "truth" to the designing of a building. The test of truth applies to every element and problem that occurs in the building and will shape its plan and section as surely as it shapes the arrangement of its smallest elements such as stone facing slabs.

Economy of means is fundamental to good building. To achieve the greatest economy of means in this century, the use of many machine-made materials is essential. In case it may be thought that this is evidence of a cheap utilitarianism, it may be pointed out here that medieval peoples had nothing but the most primitive mechanisms to help them lift and quarry their stone, and, once quarried, much of it had to be carried by pack-horse. This meant that they not only developed a wonderfully efficient small-stone technique of arches and vaults, but that they used as little stone as they could to achieve their great buildings, economising with great virtuosity, often to the point of collapse.

A Hostel for University Students

We have stated previously that buildings owe their form to the *purpose* they are to fulfil, to the *materials* at hand and to the *skill* of their builders. In this century these factors are quite different from what they were a hundred years ago. Consequently it is not surprising if contemporary buildings differ from their predecessors.

A Small House

Firstly the needs of today are very different from those of the past—our scale of values has undergone a profound change in the last century and our way of life too is quite different. The urban life led by the majority has caused a realisation of the need for sun and air in our homes. We see less reason than before for the hard and fast division between indoors and out of doors. We need to curb the sideways sprawl of the towns over our remaining agricultural land and beautiful countryside. The distinction between rich and poor, between employer and employed, is less marked than heretofore, consequently a higher standard of conditions in which most of us work and live is needed. We need different sorts of buildings that did not exist before, such as health centres and county colleges, airports, flatted factories and television studios. The impact of the motor-car on our environment is still scarcely understood, so violently and swiftly has it come. Vast new multi-storey garages will be needed above and below the ground. New highways and motorways with complicated interconnections and long elevated sections are being built. The problem of how to cater for the motor-car without destroying the character of our old cities is so difficult that no satisfactory solution has yet emerged. Where whole new towns are being designed comprehensively there is no reason whatever why proper integration should not be achieved, and architects and engineers working together can indeed solve this problem, as is being shown in new towns such as Cumbernauld near Glasgow. All these factors influence the *purpose* the buildings shall fulfil.

Secondly modern conditions, transport and

industrial techniques have made available for the builder a greatly increased variety of *materials*, some altogether new, some used in ancient times with only local application. Not only do we have the traditional materials of brick, stone and timber, but steel and concrete (the two most important), plywood and plastics, aluminium and bitumen, rubber and asbestos and many others besides. We have wholly prefabricated parts of buildings such as walls and floors because skilled people nowadays prefer to work in comfortable factory surroundings rather than on building sites which are subject to weather and are often far away from their homes. Old materials have found new forms and applications, for instance window glass has become plate-glass capable of attaining huge dimensions without support and laminated to form double glazing units capable of giving a high degree of thermal insulation; timber is laminated with modern glues not only into plywoods capable of standing up to all weathers but into beams, posts and trusses making timber capable of performing feats of strength undreamed of before.

Several results of the use of machine-made materials may be seen in modern buildings. To begin with, since the properties of these materials are exactly known, their behaviour under stress of weight or climate may be precisely calculated, so no more material than is strictly needed is used. Next, a high degree of standardisation is inevitable. Lastly, decoration is no longer a natural process, for machine-made decoration is valueless. Machine-made materials have a beauty of their own—their precision, their even texture, their economy. If the words standard, prefabricated and mass-produced have unpleasant associations, it is as well to remember that the ordinary brick has always been mass-produced and is a completely standard prefabricated article measuring 9 in. × 3 in. × 4½ in. (or rather less to allow for jointing). The same applies to roofing tiles, window glass and many other familiar building components. Today the standardisation of larger units, completely finished floors and walls for transportation to building sites for assembly in the manner of a house of cards, is becoming increasingly popular. Whole bathrooms have been delivered from factory to site ready for placing in position by crane.

It should not be supposed that all materials used in modern building must necessarily be machine made. The material best suited to the particular conditions of expedience, economy and appearance is used, and in many cases local and traditional materials still fulfil these conditions best.

Thirdly the *skill* of the builder is, of course, not only the skill of actual building contractors but also the skill required in the manufacture of their materials and factory-made products and in the design of the machines that make and move them, and also the skill of the architect and his consultant engineers—or better still of the architect-engineer partnership. Compare the skills of today in designing, manufacturing and building a modern block of offices, with its complex structure and finishes and its lifts, heating, electric light, lavatories and the rest, with the skills required in designing a medieval church of equal size. There the materials used were stone, timber, wrought iron, glass and lead—virtually no more than that. Small wonder that the care and skill lavished on these materials is held up as an example of what craftsmanship should be; and small wonder that the modern architect is at pains to simplify, for the bare necessities of his building have become so elaborate that simplification has become essential.

One further factor which has profoundly influenced modern building and the skill of the builders must be mentioned—that of communication. So well developed is our ability to communicate with one another across the world that designers can attain worldwide repute, and national differences in aesthetic and technique have virtually ceased to exist except in so far as these are influenced by different climates. For this reason we are much more influenced today by the great designers of other countries, and our modern building forms owe much to such men as the architect Le Corbusier and the famous Mexican engineer-designer Felix Candela.

The type of building that is representative of the first half of the 20th century is perhaps the small house, but as we already noted, most buildings of this period are not truly modern architecture. The Butler Education Act of 1944 which raised the school-leaving age to sixteen necessitated the building of a large number of new schools and these probably form the bulk of immediately post-war modern architecture. Latterly the rehousing of those displaced by slum clearance has produced some notable comprehensive housing developments such as those undertaken by the L.C.C. at Roehampton. Land-hunger in the centres of our cities has caused developers to build high, and until land values drop and we invent some miraculous way of feeding ourselves off a reduced agricultural acreage, skyscrapers are bound to be a continuing feature of urban central areas.

The two materials that have influenced the form of buildings more than any others are steel and concrete. These are important because they are structural rather than weatherproofing or finishing materials, and some description of the way they can be used is necessary in order that the varying shapes that modern buildings assume may be understood.

Iron was first used structurally towards the end of the 18th century, although no very remarkable feats were possible until the invention of a method of mass-producing steel. The Bessemer process was perfected during the last half of the 19th century and since then it has been possible to build very much larger and lighter buildings than before. A description of the steel-framed building has already been given. The material itself is capable of being used in this manner because it is equally strong in tension and compression, that is to say it will resist a tendency to be either crushed or pulled apart to an equal extent. In this respect it resembles timber, but is many

The Steel Frame Building

times stronger. Steel is rolled out into standard I-shaped, U-shaped, T-shaped and L-shaped sections of various sizes, the most widely used being the I-shaped. Once the frame has been set up and all the members are riveted, bolted or welded together, the walls and floors are hung on to it. Rooms and windows within the frame may be quite freely arranged, for all walls, both internal and external, are mere partitions and are quite unrelated to the structure.

The principal advantage of this strong material is that the great loads it can carry allow of considerable economy of space on the lower floors of large buildings. A multi-storey block of flats or offices, if built in solid masonry or brickwork, would have very little space left for rooms on the ground floor since so much of it would be occupied by the supporting piers. A secondary advantage is the speed with which it can be erected, for the steel is shaped and cut in the factory to fit exactly, and needs only to be hoisted into position and fixed together. The stability of external walling no longer governs the size and shape of windows and doors. A window may extend the whole length of a façade if necessary, for the beams may project beyond the columns so that the windows pass freely in front of them.

The projecting shape, or cantilever, is also well suited to reinforced concrete construction. Concrete is strong in compression—it will not crush—but it is very weak in tension, so it will crack easily if bent; in this respect it is like stone. To overcome its tensile weakness it is reinforced with steel rods. When the tension occurs in the bottom of the horizontal members the steel will be at the bottom; where in the top, the steel will be at the top. In columns the steel is like a cage to prevent the concrete bursting under the weight it bears.

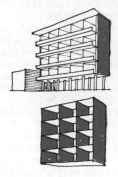

The amount of steel used and its exact positioning are calculated very accurately, and construction in this material is highly skilled work. Concrete floor slabs frequently project beyond the outside line of columns, thus enabling the windows to be of indefinite length, in the same manner as in steel-framed buildings, but in the concrete building the whole structure is homogeneous and derives much of its strength from the fact. More sophisticated methods of reinforced concrete construction are now used, such as pre-stressing and post-tensioning, where the elements of the building are artificially bent to induce a stress opposite to that which will be imposed on it in use. The effect of this is that the opposing stresses tend to cancel each other out so that the members may be made much smaller while doing the same work. Another refined technique that is employed in some buildings is that of shell construction for roofs, which can be made to span great distances when only a few inches thick. These roofs owe their strength to their subtly curved shapes and require very exacting calculation in their design. A notable example of the sort of building made possible by this development is the New Opera

A Concrete Building

House in Sydney with its sail-like shell roofs, echoing the sails of the yachts in the harbour.

From the foregoing it will have been seen that architecture today has made a break with its immediate past. The evolutionary process has taken one of those giant strides covering in a few decades ground that long ago would have been covered only during centuries of slow progress. Science, sociology and the arts have seen the same astonishing change, and architecture is at once the result and the expression of them all.

As yet modern architecture may appear austere and uncompromising, brutal or even dull. This is because the new building technique has only recently grown out of its raw infancy. Austerity may be said to be in the eye of the beholder, and is much exaggerated therein by a century and a half's conditioning in rich Victorian and Edwardian romanticism. Austerity is not a fundamental characteristic of modern architecture. The economic use of machine-made materials and of contemporary scientific structural methods are however essential results of our social structure and are no passing phase.

We hope that we have made the point that true modern architecture is not just a "style" in the sense of a decorative technique that can be applied to a building. It is the outcome of a philosophy of design which finds its roots in the social and technological revolution which western civilisation is experiencing. Modern architecture is the organisation, form, roots, structure, technology and finish not only of the building in isolation but of groups of buildings, the spaces between, the neighbourhood, the town—in fact the artificial environment of mankind.

DISTRIBUTION OF THE TRADITIONAL BUILDING MATERIALS OF GREAT BRITAIN.

SEE pp. 11—14

FLAGS

OLD AND ANCIENT ROCKS AND GRANITE

GRANITE

HIGHLAND BRITAIN
LOWLAND BRITAIN

SLATES GRANITES & SANDSTONE

CARBONIFEROUS LIMESTONE

GRANITE

GRITS SLATES AND SANDSTONES

SLATE

SLATES GRANITE SANDSTONES OLD GRITS

HARD SANDSTONES OLD GRITS

SANDY LIMESTONE

BRICKS & TIMBER

SLATE GRANITE & HARD ROCK

SLATES

TIMBER

RED SANDSTONE

BRICKS & TIMBER BELT

GREAT LIMESTONE BELT

BRICKS

BRICKS & FLINT

BRICKS AND TIMBER

GRANITE SLATE SANDSTONE

STONE

COB

BRICKS TIMBER AND FLINT HUNGTILES

Older rocks usually making hard intractable building stone.

Newer rocks usually more easily worked.

■ Igneous (Granite, etc).	■ Oolitic and Liassic Limestones
▨ Metamorphic and Ancient Sedimentaries	▨ Chalk with Flints
▦ Old Red Sandstones	▦ New Sandstone
▨ Carboniferous and Magnesian Limestones	□ Clays and Recent

HIGHLAND LINE

In most low-lying areas and valley bottoms small buildings are of timber

Norman

Norman Church (*p.* 33)

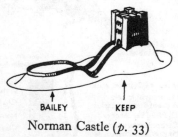

Norman Castle (*p.* 33)

Norman   *See p.* 34

Early English

Early English Cathedral (*p.* 48)

Early English Parish Church (*p.* 49)

Decorated

Decorated Cathedral (*p.* 66)

Decorated Parish Church (*p.* 62)

Perpendicular

Perpendicular Cathedral (*p.* 74)

Perpendicular Parish Church (*p.* 75)

Tudor

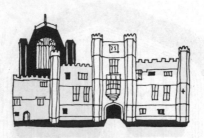

Tudor Palace (*p.* 96)

Tudor House (*p.* 102)

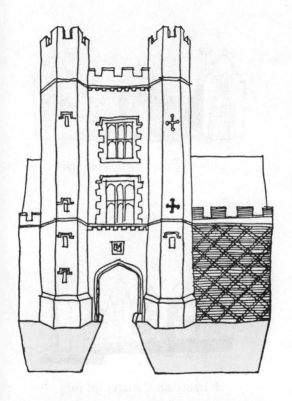

Elizabethan and Jacobean

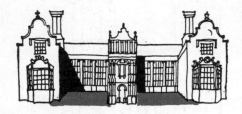

Elizabethan Mansion (*p.* 108)

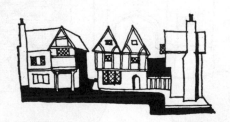

Elizabethan Cottages (*p.* 108)

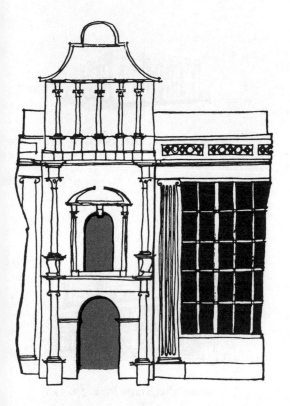

Classical

Queen's House, Greenwich (*p*. 118)

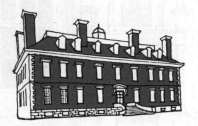

A House after Inigo Jones (*p*. 120)

Classical   *See p.* 118

181

Baroque and Queen Anne

Queen Anne House (p. 123)

Brick and Stone Combined (*p.* 121)

A Public Building (*p.* 130)

182

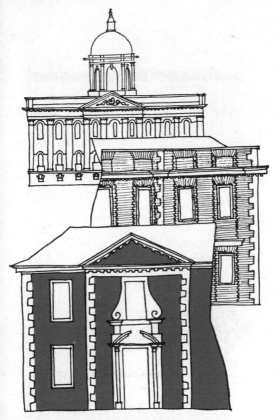

Georgian

Georgian Terrace (*p.* 135)

18th Century Crescent (*p.* 137)

184

Regency

A Nash Terrace (*p.* 143)

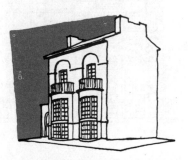

Regency Villa (*p.* 141)

186

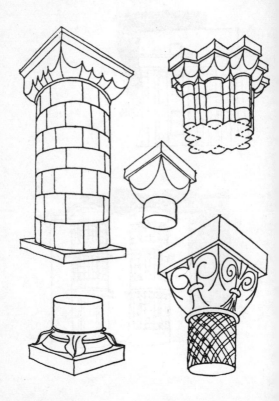

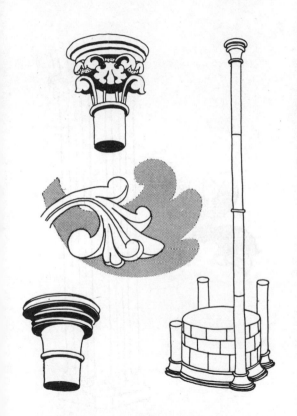

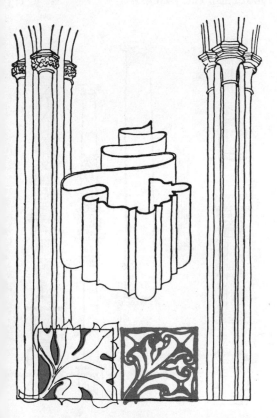

Elizabethan and Jacobean

See p. 113

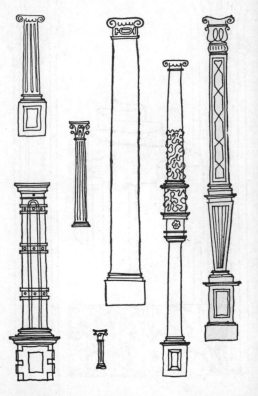

See p. 88

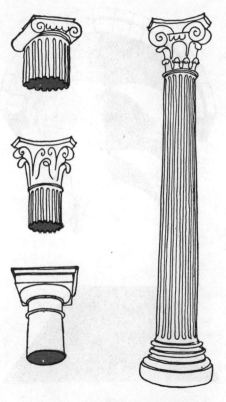

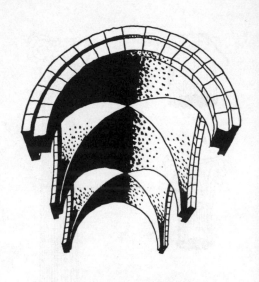

Norman and Early English

Norman
12th Century
(*see p.* 39)

Early English
13th Century
(*see p.* 55)

Decorated   *See p.* 68

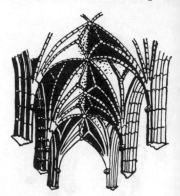

Geometrical
Patterns

Many Ribs

Perpendicular and Tudor   *See p.* 79

See p. 79

Elizabethan

See p. 114

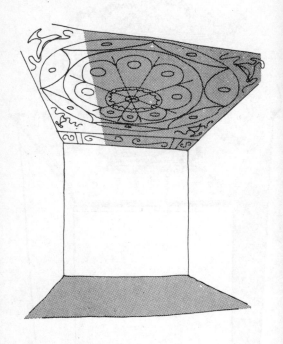

Norman and Early English

Norman
12th Century
(*see p.* 41)

Early English
13th Century
(*see p.* 58)

Decorated
14th Century
(*see p.* 70)

Perpendicular
15th Century
(*see p.* 82)

Tudor

See p. 96

Elizabethan and Jacobean See p. 112

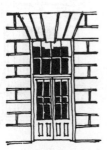

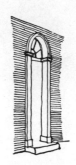

See p. 40

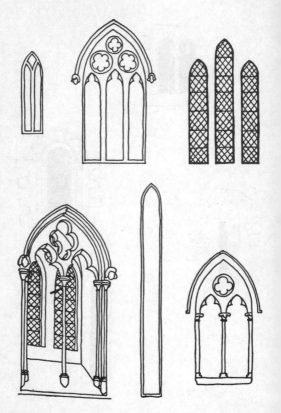

See p. 68

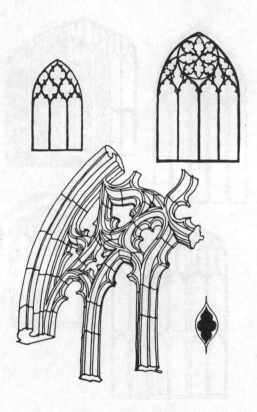

Perpendicular

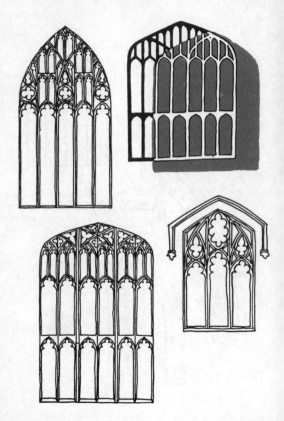

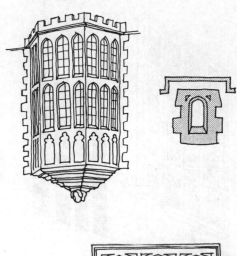

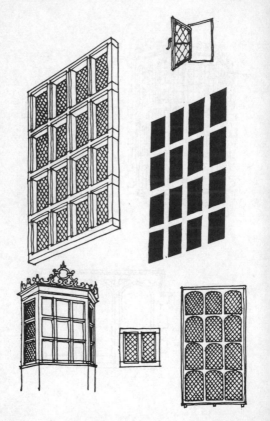

Baroque and Queen Anne   *See p.* 125

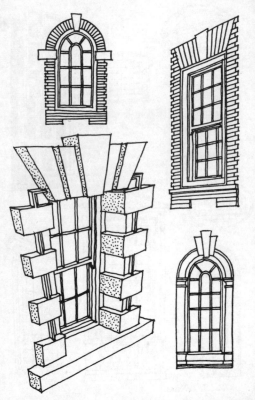

Adam and Regency

See pp. 139 *and* 144

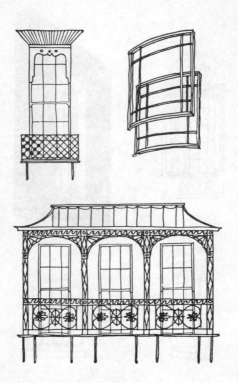

ILLUSTRATED GLOSSARY OF TERMS

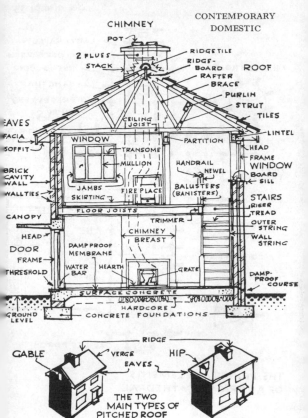

CONTEMPORARY
DOMESTIC

CHIMNEY

POT

2 FLUES

STACK

RIDGE TILE
RIDGE-
BOARD
RAFTER
BRACE
PURLIN
STRUT
TILES

ROOF

EAVES
FACIA
SOFFIT

CEILING JOIST

WINDOW

TRANSOME

MULLION

PARTITION

LINTEL
HEAD
FRAME
WINDOW
BOARD
SILL

BRICK
CAVITY
WALL

WALLTIES

HANDRAIL
NEWEL

JAMBS
SKIRTING

FIRE PLACE

BALUSTERS
(BANISTERS)

STAIRS

CANOPY

FLOOR JOISTS

TRIMMER

RISER
TREAD
OUTER
STRING
WALL
STRING

HEAD

DOOR
FRAME

THRESHOLD

DAMP PROOF
MEMBRANE

WATER
BAR

HEARTH

CHIMNEY
BREAST

GRATE

DAMP-
PROOF
COURSE

SURFACE CONCRETE

GROUND
LEVEL

HARDCORE

CONCRETE FOUNDATIONS

RIDGE

GABLE

VERGE

EAVES

HIP

THE TWO
MAIN TYPES OF
PITCHED ROOF

219

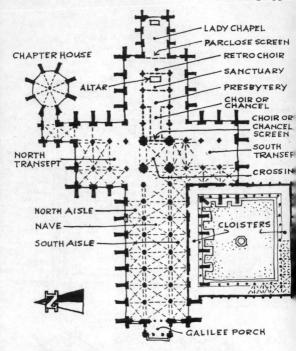

THE PRINCIPAL ELEMENTS
OF A TYPICAL CATHEDRAL

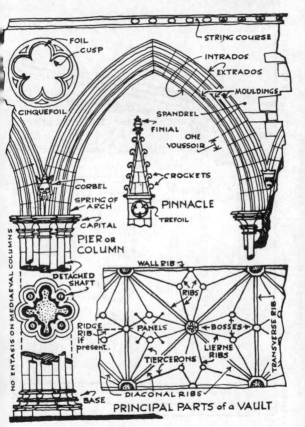

STRING COURSE

FOIL
CUSP

INTRADOS

EXTRADOS

MOULDINGS

CINQUEFOIL

SPANDREL

FINIAL

ONE
VOUSSOIR

CROCKETS

CORBEL

SPRING OF
ARCH

PINNACLE

CAPITAL

TREFOIL

PIER or
COLUMN

NO ENTASIS ON MEDIAEVAL COLUMNS

DETACHED
SHAFT

WALL RIB

RIBS

RIDGE
RIB
if
present.

PANELS

BOSSES

LIERNE
RIBS

TIERCERONS

TRANSVERSE RIB

BASE

DIAGONAL RIBS

PRINCIPAL PARTS of a VAULT

221

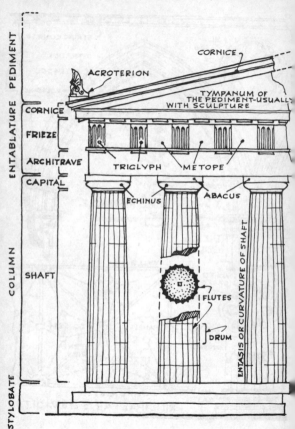

PEDIMENT

ENTABLATURE

COLUMN

STYLOBATE

CORNICE

FRIEZE

ARCHITRAVE

CAPITAL

SHAFT

CORNICE

ACROTERION

TYMPANUM OF
THE PEDIMENT—USUALL
WITH SCULPTURE

TRIGLYPH   METOPE

ECHINUS   ABACUS

FLUTES

DRUM

ENTASIS OR CURVATURE OF SHAFT

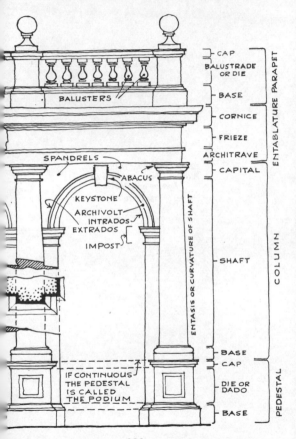

Printed in Great Britain by
William Clowes and Sons Ltd.
London and Beccles

1531.170